Light from the Angels

Now those who cannot attend the Angel Academy in person have a unique opportunity to learn about major metaphysical topics from the Angels themselves.

Light from the Angels discusses difficult subjects in the Angels' own precise, easy-to-understand language. Many formidable concepts that have been hazy for most students of metaphysics will suddenly become crystal clear and meaningful as the Angels deftly show you how life's intricate, complex puzzle pieces fit easily together.

Whether you are a professional healer, a channel, a psychic or are simply interested in advanced metaphysics, the Divine Mother and the Rose Angels will take you by the hand and lead you down exciting new pathways of self-discovery and adventure. Their methods for inner transformation are practical, appealing, and enlightening: you owe it to yourself to make them a permanent part of your spiritual life.

TOPICS INCLUDE

Making and Using Power Tools
Angelic Medicines
Healing with Dolphins
Understanding the Subtle Bodies and the Chakras
Crystals for Meditation and Healing
Building and Using Light Boxes
Achieving Deep States of Meditation
Seeing Past Lives
Finding Your Twin Soul
Reading Information Stored in the DNA
Accessing the Akashic Records
Avoiding Negativity

LIGHT FROM THE ANGELS

THE DIVINE MOTHER AND THE ROSE ANGELS
SHARE THEIR WISDOM
ON A VARIETY OF VITAL METAPHYSICAL TOPICS

Channeled through Hallie Deering for
THE ANGEL ACADEMY

Copyright © 1995 by Hallie Deering

All rights reserved.
No part of this book may
be used or reproduced in any manner
without prior written permission from
the publisher except in the case of brief
quotations embodied in critical
reviews and articles.

Cover art by
the Divine Mother
through Hallie Deering

ISBN 0-929385-72-1

Published by
Light Technology Publishing
P.O. Box 1526
Sedona, AZ
86339

Printed by
MI**SS**ION
PO**SS**IBLE
Commercial Printing
P.O. Box 1495
Sedona, AZ 86339

About the Channel

Prior to 1973 Hallie Deering taught at Colorado State University and the University of Colorado while she worked on her M.A. degree and a Ph.D. However, in January of '73 when the comet Kahoutec passed near the Earth, she underwent a sudden, profound psychic and spiritual awakening and soon found herself linked telepathically with the Angels. Shortly thereafter circumstances brought her to Sedona, where she began an intensive course of inner metaphysical study with the Divine Mother and the Rose Angels. During her Sedona years she has undergone several difficult spiritual initiations; taught metaphysical workshops on both the physical and the astral planes; performed hundreds of crystal balances and past-life regressions for lightworkers; and channeled, designed and assembled over 6000 Angelic Power Tools for professional healers around the world. She currently teaches several Angel Academy sessions per year on behalf of the Rose Angels. When she is not conducting the Angel Academy she lives in almost total seclusion, channeling books and visionary artwork for the Divine Mother and the Angels. She also writes a regular monthly column called *Angel Voices* for the *SEDONA Journal of EMERGENCE.*

About the Book

The material in this book was originally published as a series of articles from Hallie Deering's *Triple Your Healing Power* column, which appeared regularly in the *SEDONA Journal of EMERGENCE* from November of 1991 through April of 1995. The articles appear here almost verbatim, with only a few stylistic changes for the sake of continuity. There are some repetitions — most notably the Angelic Master Meditation Technique — which were left in for the reader's convenience.

The columns that comprise this book were written at the request of the Divine Mother and the Rose Angels, who chose the topics for each month, suggested ways to approach each subject, telepathically dictated some of the wording for the most difficult concepts, and left the rest up to the channel. Consequently the column is a combination of material from the Divine Mother and the Angels mixed with the comments and personal experiences of the channel, with occasional reference to classical metaphysical authors.

CONTENTS

The Holy Mother, the Angels, and the Academy

1. Songs of the Divine Mother 1
2. The Rose Angels and the Angel Academy 9

Topics of General Interest

3. A Metaphysical Christmas 15
4. The View from the Stargate 19

A Wealth of Angelic Healing Methods

5. Power Tools: Angelic Technology Brought to Earth 27
6. Angelic Medicines 35
7. Healing with Elegance 41
8. Gathering Information Before a Healing Session 47
9. Healing with Rainbows 53
10. Rose-Colored Glasses 57
11. If You Don't Feel It, You Can't Heal It 61
12. Hands That Heal 65
13. Healing with Dolphins 71
14. The Subtle Bodies: What They Are and How They Work . . 75
15. Understanding the Chakras 81
16. The Death Experience: Making the Big Transition 87
17. Resurrection on the Astral Plane 93

Using Crystals for Healing and Meditation

18. Gifts from the Angels 101
19. Choosing the Right Crystals 105
20. Making a Master Healing Crystal 111
21. Build Your Own Vortex 115
22. Three Excellent Crystal Balances 121
23. Crystals as Fragments of the Divine Mind 129

Meditation for Healing And Transformation

24. Be Sure of Your Inner Guidance 139
25. The Joys of Meditation 143
26. The Angels' Master Meditation Technique 149
27. Several Auxiliary Meditation Techniques 157
28. Advanced Meditation Techniques 165
29. Past Life Trauma 171
30. Beginning the Search for Past Life Trauma 175
31. Seeing Past Lives 183
32. Finding Your Twin Soul 191
33. Three Useful Meditations 197
34. Reactivating the Immune System 201
35. Reading DNA Memories 205
36. Using the Akashic Records 213

Coping with Negativity

37. Avoiding Nightmares 221
38. Building an Auric Shield 225

THE HOLY MOTHER,
THE ANGELS,
AND THE
ACADEMY

1

Songs of the Divine Mother

Many people have written asking about the Divine Mother, and since this is my favorite topic, let's use this month's column to see how meditation on the Divine Mother can make your life infinitely sweeter. If you have been following this column regularly, you already know the clear simplicity of the Divine Mother's thoughts because much of what I write comes directly from her. I have hesitated to write about the Divine Mother from my own viewpoint for the simple reason that she is so deliciously overwhelming that there just didn't seem to be words to describe her. But it seems that now is the time to at least try to summarize some of the things I have seen throughout the many incarnations I have spent meditating on her.

Her Outer Forms

The Divine Mother is of the Angelic Kingdom, but she has incarnated many times on this planet in human form. When she incarnates she does it just like you and I do, without memory of who she is on the higher planes or where she comes from. She never picks an easy incarnation; her reasoning is that if we have to go through great difficulty, so will she. Is she incarnate on Earth today? I strongly, strongly suspect she is, perhaps in many bodies but almost certainly in the form of Mother Teresa. There is a channeled portrait of the Divine Mother in Geoffrey Hodson's book on Angels, *The Kingdom of Gods.* If you have seen a picture of Mother Teresa, you will note the strong resemblance in the look and style of the clothing and the way it is worn. Also, Mother Teresa's selfless lifestyle, spiritual outlook on life and tireless work are so similar to those of the Divine Mother that there doesn't seem to be much room for doubt as to who is inhabiting that form. I have a card with Mother Teresa's signature on it; when held to the third eye, it has a remarkably cool, refreshing sensation, even on a hot desert day.

In addition to her many incarnations, the Divine Mother has appeared in visions to people of all religions. She is Ishtar, Isis, Parvati, Demeter, Ceres, Kwan Yin, White Buffalo Calf Woman and Mary, to name just a few. When she appears to people in this way, her outer form usually matches their own. She will appear black to a black person, Asian to an Eastern person and so on. Her clothing is usually some form of the person's national dress: Babylonian, Egyptian, Celtic and so on. Her age seems indeterminate in many of these visions — one minute when she is laughing she will appear to be about thirty, the next minute, when she is giving spiritual counsel, she will appear to be older. No matter which form she takes, she is always enchanting beyond words.

Her Inner Forms

When she appears to you in your personal meditations, the Divine Mother takes on a unique and very dear form which she assumes just for you, and for you alone. This is what you would call her inner form. When you see her in this form, you will recognize her instantly.

Her inner form is always one of dazzlingly radiant Light, warmth, serenity and beauty. The first face you beheld as your soul came into creation was the blessed face of the Divine Mother, which is exquisite beyond description. As you stand in her presence on the finer planes between earthly incarnations and gaze into her splendid eyes you suddenly notice the intoxicating scent of flowers. An overwhelming love flows into your heart, a deep, aching, healing love that comes from her through you and out to every living creature. Your soul expands with bliss as it radiates this love back to her. Your mind fills with the most glorious sound: it's the Divine Mother singing to you, and as you listen to her sweet, poignant song, you begin to experience cosmic consciousness.

Every place, every thing, every molecule seems to be made of brilliant light and soft sound. You see the harmonies of vast universes, all moving in perfect kaleidoscopic synchronization, and you are part of this infinite, perfect whole. In a state of bliss you float through endless realms of love and light. Close beside you during all of this is your beloved Divine Mother, and she shows you sights such as your soul is longing to see: pristine landscapes untouched by pollution that you can roam at will, and that energize your spirit as you are constantly delighted by new and wondrous scenes; great angelic cities of light where beings of light congregate; sights of such Angels, Saints and Masters that your soul reels to witness the unique degree of love and devotion that radiates from each one.

What does your heart desire? The Divine Mother knows, and

she will gift you with it, in overwhelming abundance. She will heal every wound, she will fulfill every wish. She will understand your most inexpressible thoughts — your agonies, your triumphs, your disappointments, your worries, your guilts, your fears, your illnesses, your pains, your doubts, your hopes, your passions, your goals, your daydreams. You will realize that this world is nothing more than a little schoolroom where past mistakes are as valuable to your spiritual development as are right decisions and noble deeds. It's all just experience in its myriad forms, and each of us has to do it all and see it all before we move on.

You will see that the Divine Mother has always been right beside you throughout all of infinity. She stands beside you as you go through the trials and tribulations of life; she brings you love and solace as you sleep at night; she helps you carry every burden; she sends you spiritual nourishment each day; she weeps with you and laughs with you. She sends you friends to help and care for you in your everyday life. She rejoices in you because you are one of a kind. Only you can be you, and she treasures you for being who you are. She loves you for the Light that you bring to the world, for your patience and perseverance. She never judges you, she is *never* negative, angry or critical; she always understands you to the very depths of your being.

The Divine Mother is your dearest, most beloved friend. She is the truest of the true, and she is *always* there for you. No problem is too large or too small to share with her. She can guide you surely and safely through every difficulty. She loves you with a love greater than you can possibly imagine, and she asks nothing in return. Simply reach out in meditation and take hold of her hand. She is, always has been, and always will be right here beside you.

Meditation Techniques

Coming into the presence of the Divine Mother is like walking out into a warm spring day after a bitterly harsh winter. Tears of joy will pour down your face the first time you recognize her in deep meditation. You will float through life on a pink cloud for weeks, months, and years after the experience. Your heart chakra will expand to fill your meditation room, your house and beyond.

The basic meditation techniques that you will need to see her are found in the meditation section of this book. Simply get into your gold body, climb your pyramid of light and go to your own special place. From there, call to the Divine Mother in your heart, inviting her to your meditation place. She will instantly be there, but it is up to you to perceive her. Watch and listen carefully. She might appear in a haze until your daily meditation is fine-tuned enough to perceive her inner form, and then she will appear in a blaze of light and soft beauty. Look for her every time you meditate in your special place — and remember, she is subtle and it requires concentration and perseverance.

Listening to Music

If you are more clairaudient than clairvoyant, or even if you're not, this is a magical technique. You have all heard tales of how the Angels sing, and it is true. The sound is sublime beyond your wildest expectations. What most people don't know is that many, many of the most wondrous angelic singers have incarnated on Earth to share with us their magnificent abilities. Most of the female angelic singers channel the Divine Mother with their voices, flooding each song with heavenly melodies and psychic nuances that can be heard only in a state of deep meditation. Invariably such singers become world famous, since subconsciously we all respond to the Divine Mother's voice when it is channeled in this way.

If you have earphones, use them for this meditation, because you need to pick up on subtleties. If you don't have earphones, try sitting between the two speakers of your sound system.

As above, begin by climbing the pyramid in your gold body and going to your special place. Then listen intently to any of the following women — I have heard the Divine Mother clearly channeling through all of their voices many times: try arias by Beverly Sills, Joan Sutherland or Kiri Te Kanawa; or anything whatsoever by (brace yourself, these are old-timers) Doris Day, Patti Page, Dinah Shore, Patsy Cline or Julie Andrews. If you're not into excavating old music, try Enya and, above all, give Nana Mouskouri a listen — she is pure magic. You can find her at Tower Records under Female Vocalists or International (Greece, generally, although she sings in many countries and many languages). Ten years ago this lady had about 170 international gold records; by now she probably has double that number. She sings all kinds of music, from folk to popular to country to jazz to classical, so there will surely be something to suit your tastes.

As you listen to your chosen music, visualize the Divine Mother sitting right there in front of you in your special place. Imagine that the voice you hear is hers and that she is singing specifically to you. The Divine Mother will then put pictures, emotions, and thoughts into your mind using the nuances of the singer's voice. This special type of channeling is hard to describe and difficult to get the hang of, but it's well worth the effort. And it will be a truly electric moment when you perceive the Divine Mother's thought within the singer's voice for the first time. The words to the songs are sometimes relevant, but generally not, except for a little phrase here and there. It's the nuances of emotion that count the most.

In Your Dreams

Have you ever had a dream like this? The astral night is cold, there's a creepy feeling in the air. Bizarre, unpleasant things are happening. If you have, tell yourself each night before you go to bed that when you have such nightmares on the astral plane you can always call on the Divine Mother to come to your aid. If you let her, she will enter into your astral dream space and guide you to safety.

If you have been meditating regularly on the Divine Mother, she will also sometimes appear to you in a wondrous astral experience that you will remember as an especially enchanting dream. When this happens, you will know she was with you!

The Divine Mother can be your constant companion if you wish her to be. You can call on her mentally at any time of the day or night and she will be there instantly. Not only is she exquisite to behold, but she is also practical. She will help you achieve strength and stability spiritually, mentally, emotionally and physically, and she will help you find simple solutions to complex problems. But she will also help you plan a menu, find your car keys, remember a friend's birthday, tough out an illness, make a garden, give a party, find help when your car quits on the highway, design a house, build a business or whatever else is of concern to you at any given moment of your life. You will soon find that she has a surprising, elfin sense of humor and a sparkling, cheerful, ever-optimistic personality. She will turn every day into a special day, and she will touch your life in a million ways.

The Divine Mother is your beloved friend, teacher, advisor and spiritual guide.

You have known her always and she is always, always, *always* right here watching over you, today, tomorrow and for all of infinity.

2

The Rose Angels
and the Angel Academy

In the crystal-clear energy of the finer planes one can some-times catch a glimpse of the exquisite angelic City of Light shining with overwhelming splendor. The sight of the city warms the heart and lifts the spirit.

Within the radiant city is a wondrous University built of colored marble, quartz and all manner of gemstones. The sight of the University awakens the third eye and crown chakras.

The University is run by the Divine Mother and the Rose Order of Angels. The Divine Mother is truly the eternal, greatly beloved mother of us all; the Rose Angels are incarnations of love and wisdom as well as healers and teachers. Their outer auras look like huge flames constantly flashing and flaring a thousand shades of bright rose and gold light; their inner forms are beautiful beyond imagining.

Congregated at the University are Spiritual Masters and their student initiates from all walks of life, from all the various peoples of the universe, from all dimensions. They are here in the spirit of peace and harmony, for the purposes of attaining true wisdom and using it to help humankind and their various home worlds.

At this time the angelic University is preparing to open a small extension on the physical plane, right here in Sedona among the powerful vortex energy fields.

The Angel Academy

The extension is called the Angel Academy and it will meet in Sedona several times a year. There will be one or two AngelFire sessions whose goal is to learn all about Angels and get students and healers up (*way* up) and running at nearly full spiritual capacity, and there will be a Crystal Camp session that deals with the fine art of using crystals and gems for personal spiritual advancement and for healing purposes. The third session is the Master Key class, which offers very deep meditation and mind-travel techniques designed to greatly strengthen each student's links with the finer planes and most especially with the University and its celestial staff. The Master Key session also teaches many highly advanced mental healing techniques.

Each student will work with the Divine Mother, a special Angel Companion, and one or more Spiritual Masters. Every session is intensive, lasting from 9 a.m. until 9 p.m. for five days.

Morning classes of each session are for receiving fascinating, detailed channeled wisdom from the Angels.

Afternoons are spent in the vortices practicing what has been learned. In addition, each student will make two Power Tools with his/her Angel Companion and pair up with a classmate in order to work on each other with Power Tools and crystals. There will also be free time for meals and shopping in Sedona's metaphysical stores.

Evenings fly by quickly as each student shares the day's happenings and insights with classmates. In this way each person benefits from the experiences of everyone else, allowing everyone to learn at an accelerated rate. Later, after students have gone to bed, the Angels will pull them out of their bodies and take them astral-projecting in the vortices.

At the completion of each session, each student is presented with an Angel Academy certificate of achievement, suitable for framing in the home or place of spiritual work.

Yours Truly, Coming from The Heart

I am delighted to say that it will be my very great pleasure to teach all of the sessions. I look forward to meeting many old friends from this life, other dimensions, former incarnations, and hopefully many new friends as well. I promise you a totally authentic experience with the most wonderful guides imaginable. You will be intrigued, fascinated and exhilarated. You will laugh, and many of you will weep for happiness. And when your session is over you will feel an enormous sense of confidence in the Angels, in who you are, and in what you have learned.

The tuition for each Academy session is $500 for a five-day class, plus $50 for an Angel ToolKit, which contains the supplies you will need to make your Power Tools and carry out class assignments. Over 60% of the Angel Academy profits go to charitable foundations that better our spiritual lives, fight for animal rights, work to save the planet's ecology, and help the poor, the starving and the dying. The other 40% goes toward computer equipment, printing, advertising, conference room rental and class supplies, and toward providing me with enough money to meet my personal needs, which are generally small.

Read All About It

A very exciting 16-page, full-color booklet on the Angel

Academy is now available. If you are meant to attend the Academy, you will know it when you see the booklet: angelic energy literally pours off every page, and those who are the most ready for the experience will feel as if they are receiving a personal invitation directly from the Angels. I am asking $1 for this booklet to help defray postage and the cost of printing in full color: you will find that as a spiritual document its value is far, far higher than the $1 price. To send for your booklet, please *print* your name and address and send $1 to: The Angel Academy, 2610 Jacks Canyon Road, Sedona, AZ 86351, or call (520) 284-1550.

We're Off to See the Angels . . .

In the full Light of Spirit the Divine Mother, the Rose Angels, the many Spiritual Masters and I also send you heartfelt greetings and deep joy. We all look forward to seeing *you* at the Angel Academy.

TOPICS OF
GENERAL INTEREST

3

A Metaphysical Christmas

As Christmas day approaches, those of you who are meditating up into the finer planes will no doubt notice that there is a wondrous sparkle to the higher energies, and that a lot of this special energy is flowing down to the physical plane in ever-increasing amounts. These energies can be clearly felt on our physical level as that special love, generosity, zest and exhilaration which traditionally permeate the Christmas season. On a more inward level, as you sit quietly to meditate you will notice that your heart energy feels saturated with brightly colored light, and expansive with the grace of the spirit of pure outward-directed love. These uplifting energies are being poured upon the Earth at this time by the various members of the Angelic Kingdom.

The Angels at Christmas

The Angels have been Earth's closest neighbors for as long as there has been an Earth. Angels coexist with us on this planet and they spend a great deal of their time in loving service to humanity. Christmas and Easter are two of the most joyous seasons for all of Earth's many Angels, and at these special times they literally deluge the Earth with angelic energies. Regular holiday meditation in this energy is like sitting amidst huge chasms of radiant, multicolored light.

O Christmas Tree

Have you ever wondered just what the significance of a Christmas tree really is? Try thinking of your spinal column as the trunk of a tree, and the many nerve bundles coming off the spine as the tree's branches.

Imagine kundalini energy flowing up your spine, lighting your auric field with a million dazzling sparkles of Light. The star at the top of the tree represents a spiritual symbol that is found in the aura over the forehead of those who are awakened into cosmic (Christ) consciousness. And the Angel at the very top of the tree is your Guardian Angel floating high above you, watching over you, guiding and protecting you.

Reach for the Sky: A Special Christmas Balance

Those of you who do healing work — or even those who would just like to help a friend or family member — will find that this is a very good time to open, clean and balance your clients' or friends' heart, throat, third eye and crown chakras so these higher spiritual centers can receive maximum benefit from the angelic energies that flow during the month of December. (The same holds true for the Easter season also.)

Try putting a clear quartz crystal point up on your client's or friend's crown chakra, a small one on the brow chakra — also pointing up — the same at the throat, and four clear quartz crystals on the heart chakra in a cross formation. Pointing the four crystals inward will bring the angelic energies into the heart; switching them so they point outward halfway though the session will flow the energy through the heart chakra and out to loved ones. If you can, find a nice crystal to put in the center of the four — amethyst and rose quartz are nice; ruby and emerald are sublime. If you are working with Power Tools, put an appropriate disk at each of the four upper chakras instead of crystals, or use both crystals and Power Tools.

If you have a crystal necklace or pendulum, swirl it above the heart chakra in a clockwise motion, then do the same above the throat, third eye and crown chakras. Now raise your left hand high above your head with the palm up, and put your right hand palm down over your client's heart chakra, about three inches above the body. Close your eyes and feel your left palm begin to tingle or heat up as your Guardian Angel pours energy down into your body. Pull this energy from your left palm through your arm into your heart chakra, push it down your right arm, through the crystals or Power Tools and into your client's heart chakra. Remember yourself in a past life as a Priest or Priestess of Light, and treat this act as a sacrament. As you come from this special place, the energy will flow through you in huge quantities. Repeat the process at the throat, third eye and crown chakras. If your client or friend is the least bit clairvoyant, he or she should definitely feel this. If he or she is *very* clairvoyant, it is possible to see the Guardian Angel at work.

A Voice for Those Who Have No Voice

If you want to see an Angel cry, tune in to any Angel in the vicinity of a Christmas tree lot. All Angels love trees dearly: trees are lovely spiritual entities who make life on this planet possible and are homes for many small animals. For the Angels it is a huge distress to see these young, beautiful, conscious spiritual beings slaughtered by the millions merely for the sake of symbolism. If you are still using a real tree at Christmas, consider switching to a good artificial tree or using a living tree and transplanting it into your yard or any other appropriate place. Each living tree is invaluable to the Earth's atmosphere, and older trees form large, beautiful vortices of uplifting spiritual energies. If you really want to get into the Christmas tree spirit, find the biggest old pine tree you can and meditate at the foot of it. As you sit, the tree will fill your aura with life-giving prana, and if you are clairvoyant or clairaudient you can actually contact the tree's spirit. I have planted a lot of pine trees on my property, and have felt their pleasure as I sprayed them with cool water on a hot day and their gratitude when I turn on their drip system or give them their spring or fall nutrients. It's touching to see their joy when a bird or chipmunk sits among their branches. They are a beautiful sight every day of the year, and the prana they produce gives my land a mellow glow. The thought of killing one of them just for the sake of symbolism and then throwing it away after a week is inexpressibly sad. So please, on behalf of the Angels and the Earth itself and all of us, help save the trees!

Christmas Blessings

The Divine Mother and all of the Angels — and most especially the healing Angels who assist you with your daily healing work — send you their most heartfelt wishes for a deeply meaningful holiday season and the dawn of a wonderful and exciting new spiritual day. And of course my own blessings are with you also. Have a splendid Christmas!

4

The View from the Stargate

As I write this it is mid-December 1995, and the 12:12 energy has just begun to flow. The Divine Mother has told me so many exciting and wonderful things about the significance of this time that I would like to pass the information on to you. When you read this the energies should be higher, stronger and smoother than they are now and the following information should be easy to confirm in meditation.

The Pleiadean Stargate

Just as every country, state and county has a capitol city, so does our universe. This is in fact the origin of the word *university:* universe city. The prime city of our universe is located in the Pleiadean system, and it is called the angelic City of Light. (You will perhaps remember that I spoke of this city in last month's column.) The City of Light is filled with Angels, ambassadors, envoys, spiritual and political leaders, teachers, students, scientists, healers, and citizens from every known part of the universe. It is a wondrous place, and we all have memories of it encoded into our DNA.

The Earth is always monitored by our colleagues in the City, but the connection is somewhat faint and difficult to perceive from our dense physical forms, surrounded as we are by the chaotic vibrations of Earth. However, from time to time we come into an especially strong alignment with the Pleiades and the City of Light; when this special alignment happens, a huge stargate opens. This Pleiadean Stargate has opened many times before, but only for a duration of several hours or days. During such times the Earth is flooded with psychic information coming to us from the City of Light, which generally leads to huge leaps forward in the realms of our science, technology, political stability, humanitarian concepts and so on. The Industrial Revolution is a good example of the results of the opening of the Pleiadean Stargate, as is our current computer age.

What is so exciting about the 12:12 is that it marks the reopening of the Pleiadean Stargate, and this time the gate will stay open for many years. This is why so many lightworkers are now incarnate and conscious on deep levels: so we can receive the veritable flood of information that is to come, and then play our parts in anchoring this information onto the planet in a variety of forms, according to our individual talents and skills. We lightworkers have come in huge numbers to all parts of the globe, just waiting for this particular stargate to open; we are channels, healers, teachers, writers, artists, musicians, entertainers, filmmakers, scientists, politicians, farmers, gridworkers, nutritionists, ecologists . . . the list goes on and on.

The First Energies

The gate was due to open on December 12 between noon and

midnight; early in the afternoon the alignment snapped into focus, and by 9 p.m. the first glimmerings of lovely energy were beginning to be felt. I should emphasize that this energy comes to us from our colleagues from all over the universe who are stationed in the City of Light, so it is not strictly an angelic or a Pleiadean energy; it is an amalgam of broad-spectrum universal energies that are being focused and channeled through the Pleiadean Stargate.

By midnight the energy was chaotic, flowing much the same way water does when the floodgates of a dam are opened: universal energies poured and churned into the earth's atmosphere like a flash flood racing down a dry ravine. While we slept that first night we received entirely new programming, which washed through our DNA like a refreshing rain after a long drought.

After a few days (I write this on the 20th) the energy has smoothed out somewhat, and our colleagues on the Pleiadean side of the stargate are standing by, waiting to work with us as soon as the light shifts during the winter solstice on the 21st. Many of us have already been assigned to several study groups for orientation and advanced learning on the higher planes. We will meet with these groups almost every night from now on, as the energy builds and begins to work its magic.

Glimmerings of What Is to Come

This is truly it, my friends! This is what we have all been waiting for, and it is well under way. As you read this many of you are probably already very active on the astral (and higher) planes at night, and most of you are probably aware of an exhilarating new energy coming into your daily lives. In addition to the new DNA programming, a lot of personal information that has been in your DNA but unavailable to you is now being brought up to the level of your conscious awareness.

Many of you will notice your diet, work, home life and spiritual life undergoing strong changes for the better. You may be suddenly heading in awesome, inspiring new directions and knowing things at a much deeper level. And your emotions may be overflowing in a very positive way. The hectic rush of ups and downs that affected most of us before Christmas should now be slowing down somewhat, and as you settle into a more comfortable, fulfilling lifestyle, the spiritual nourishment for which we have all hungered will be flowing to you in generous measure.

Old and new friends will come to you, and these relationships will be intensified and much more meaningful. Unfortunately, you may also find that people who had seemed to be friends will suddenly become hostile, sullen and angry. Let these people go; their paths lie elsewhere, and they have their own very serious karmic lessons to learn and karmic debts to pay.

A Word to Healers

As healers, most of us have been clearing old junk intensively for years, and now is the time to begin helping others with their own deep-level clearing. As new information is seeded into your clients' DNA, many will begin to throw off old, archaic limitations and illnesses. You will probably find many of your clients going through extremely profound releases as you work on them, and your own past clearing experiences will provide excellent insights as to how to help them.

You might also find yourself drawn anew to collect special crystals; to read new books; to work with herbs or flower and gem essences; to experiment with new healing methods and styles; and to travel to spiritual centers such as Sedona, Egypt or Peru. Your psychic intuition is likely to bring to your conscious attention many new techniques that you are learning on the finer planes at night. You will probably find that you are considerably more sensitive to your clients, able to pick up clues and hunches regarding the origins of their problems at a much deeper level than ever before, and as a result your clientele will probably expand considerably.

Many healers make very little money, but the Divine Mother emphasizes that you are entitled to ask a reasonable fee for your work. You will be earning it, and many of you will be needing to buy crystals and other items to supplement your work. The time for poverty is past. Also, be good to yourself during these times: healing work requires huge amounts of energy, so stay well fed on healthy food, be relaxed and get plenty of sleep, exercise and outdoor time. If you have difficulty relaxing on this tense planet, try wearing a piece of lepidolite at the heart level, perhaps in a shirt pocket or as a necklace.

An Endless Upward Spiral

I do not yet know how long the Pleiadean Stargate will remain open, but it will be at least 15 years and perhaps 30, giving us all a great deal of time to initiate many deeply meaningful changes for the Earth and her people, and for ourselves as well. And so the adventure begins, as we work our way eternally onward and upward in a beautiful spiritual spiral!

A WEALTH OF
ANGELIC HEALING
METHODS

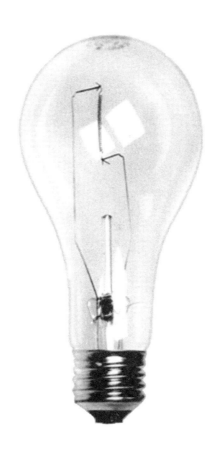

5

Power Tools: Angelic Technology Brought to Earth

ower Tools are angelic instruments for healing, channeling
and clairvoyance. They represent a highly advanced level
of mental and spiritual technology that is widely used and re-
spected throughout the finer planes. For the first time this wonderful technology is now being channeled from the angelic temples
down to the physical dimension for the use of professional healers,
channels and anyone in metaphysics who is interested in moving
at an accelerated pace.

Basically, Power Tools are flat, thick glass disks which are
placed on the chakras. Each Power Tool is basically an interdi-

mensional window which channels angelic energy down to the earth plane. There are currently three main types of Power Tools: the Metallic Disks, the Temple Jewels, and the Holographic Disks. The Angel Academy teaches its students to make the Metallic Disks and the Temple Jewels, and this book also has a chapter on making Temple Jewels (see Chapter 21, Build Your Own Vortex). The Holographic Disks are available in the form of do-it-yourself books which contain the designs for several disks. Each of the holographic disk designs consists of a photographic-quality scene or image in bright, semitransparent colors. These scenes and images are solidified thought forms.

Thought Forms

As most students of metaphysics know, thoughts are very real, very forceful things . . . they can hurt, or they can heal; they can chain us down, or they can give us a spectacular mental and spiritual escape from our mundane surroundings.

Whenever we are thinking with concentration, our thoughts *literally* appear above our heads in the form of little holograms. Thought holograms are formed from the energies of the astral, mental and causal planes (the mental plane is just above the astral in terms of vibration; the causal is above the mental). These super high-vibrational holographic manifestations of the mind's energy are called *thought forms*. As we think, a steady stream of thought forms is projected from our higher bodies; these holograms are clearly visible to many people who have inner vision.

Thought forms are extremely potent, and can actually take on a life force of their own, especially when directed by a clear mind and firm will. When a thought form has been created to help another person, it leaves the thinker's auric field and flies straight to the person it is to help: when it comes into contact with that person, it penetrates his or her aura and discharges its energy into the auric field. If the thought form is of an exceptionally high-vibrational spiritual or healing character, once it has lodged into the auric field it becomes a wonderful dynamic force for change — protecting, defending, uplifting, balancing, healing and energizing the recipient on every possible level. Angels and other spiritual Masters frequently send such sophisticated thought forms to their students for the purposes of healing, attunement, self-realization, spiritual enlightenment and finer-plane initiations.

Since our very beings are the thought forms of the Creator, it is readily apparent that healing thought forms are potentially one of the fastest, easiest and most powerful ways to modify and evolve ourselves. This is especially true when the thought forms are produced by healing Angels.

For lightworkers from the peaceful higher dimensions, Power Tools are like life-giving water in the desert, bringing magical holographic energies from the angelic plane to help restore our spiritual connections and our physical well-being.

The Images

Since thought itself is infinite, thought forms are equally unlimited in scope and possibility. Consequently there are many different holographic types of Power Tools serving a wide variety of spiritual and metaphysical purposes. There are Power Tools that portray healing plants and herbs and carry their energy; Power Tools with geometric designs to open, balance and tune the chakras; Power Tools with portraits of Ascended Masters and Angels; Power Tools that impact the DNA; Power Tools for reading past-life memories and the Akashic Records; Power Tools for channeling; Power Tools for protection from negativity; and Power Tools for cleansing and healing the auric field as well as the physical and subtle bodies, to name just a few.

Power Tools are characterized by their accurate portrayal of the scenery and inhabitants of the physical, astral, mental and causal planes. Just how precise are these scenes? Each and every Power Tool image is edited at a resolution of 9,000 dots per square inch, which is *substantially* more detailed than thought forms produced by the human mind. In addition, each Power Tool is printed in bright, rich colors which send their healing frequencies deeply into the body.

Power Tools accurately reproduce the very highest spiritual vibrations of the gems, flora, fauna and spiritual beings portrayed on them. This means if you have a disk with a Master on it, *the Master's energy actually flows through the disk.*

The same holds true for the healing energies of the Angels, plants, gems, and everything else that is portrayed on the various Power Tools.

It should be noted that the term "Holographic Disk" does not mean that the picture itself is a hologram, but that the disk transfers its image into the recipient's auric field in a form of an astral, mental or causal hologram.

Using Power Tools

Because light is the medium used to transfer spiritual energy into the disks, light also plays a vital role in transferring the energy from the disks into the user's auric field. The disks are, in fact, specifically designed to be used with a strobe light, because it is the pulsating rhythm of the strobe that carries a Power Tool's image quickly and deeply into the aura. Radio Shack sells a medium-sized strobe light for about $35 and a small, hand-held jogger's strobe for about $20. The astonishing results a strobe produces make it well worth the investment. *Please remember, however, to never ever strobe a person with epilepsy.*

If no strobe is available, the disks are used with ordinary lamp light for a longer time. The average time needed to transfer a disk's image into the auric field is two to three minutes with a strobe light, or about twenty minutes without a strobe.

Most people feel strong bolts of energy as they hold Power Tools: when the disks are strobed on their chakras, extraordinary things begin to happen very quickly.

During a Power Tool session, especially if a strobe is used, the image on each disk is perfectly reproduced as a hologram in the recipient's aura, where it shines with great beauty as it begins its work of healing, balancing, energizing,and evolving. Although the auric effects of one session can last for several weeks, the more times a disk is used, the more potent its effect will be as it becomes a permanent part of the recipient's aura.

Power Tools are especially wonderful in combinations. Using different disks on several or all of the chakras at the same time produces a truly intense healing session, helping you find, unravel, and understand every possible ramification of a problem.

Power Tools work extremely well with virtually all other healing techniques such as massage, Reiki, crystals, hands-on, psychotherapy and the like, as well as with guided meditation tapes, flower essences, gem elixirs, aroma therapy, toning, crystal bowls, Tibetan bells, classical or New Age music and the like.

After a deep Power Tool session using the channeled techniques that come with the disks, many people experience profound feelings of release and exhilaration, a crystal-clear state of consciousness, deepened moments of self-awareness, keen past-life recall, and sometimes a rush of spiritual devotion that borders on ecstasy. In short, Power Tools are definitely the genuine article.

Lightworkers from many parts of the world work with Power Tools, and they all have an abundance of tales to tell about the truly profound miracles the disks have brought into their lives and into the lives of their family, friends, and clients.

How Power Tools Are Made

Power Tools are channeled directly from the Divine Mother (who is of angelic origin) and a group of healing Angels who specialize in thought forms. As a result of centuries of exacting study and mental discipline, these beautiful, gentle Angels are able to create very intricate, precise thought forms which radiate Divine Grace.

In order to bring the highly detailed angelic thought forms

down to our physical plane, the original Power Tools were channeled from the Angels down to me: I then carefully reproduced
each image using advanced computer technology, printed it on
transparent film, and then assembled anywhere from two to four
layers of transparencies by hand into disk form.

Since the above process is very exacting, tedious, and slow, I
was able to make only a few hundred Power Tools per year for the
use of those whose inner guidance led them to the disks. After a
few years, however, orders were flooding in from all over the
world, and it became impossible for me to fill them all. I was
working on Power Tools all day every day, and basically I had no
life and no time to channel new designs. When I was finally about
to collapse from exhaustion, I had to discontinue Power Tools
altogether. But the demand for them did not go away!

Eventually the Angels reached a wonderful compromise: they
decided to publish books of do-it-yourself Power Tools that each
lightworker could assemble for her/himself. I still channel the
designs of the Power Tools, but they are printed commercially on
very thin, transparent paper instead of acetate, which makes them
about 80% easier to produce and assemble. Since I no longer have
to do the printing, or put together and mail every disk myself, or
buy huge quantities of glass and copper foil, this means you can
buy a Power Tool book with several designs for far less than the
price of one of the old Power Tools. So by assembling them
yourself with a few inexpensive supplies from your stained glass
shop, you can get many more Power Tools for your money.

Purchasing Power Tools

Power Tool books contain the designs for about 10 Holographic Power Tools . They include detailed instructions on how
to assemble each disk and how to use it. The first book is due to
be released by Easter 1995. If all goes as planned, at least one new
Power Tool book will be published each year thereafter.

You may order all Angel Academy books — including Power

Tool books — through Light Technology. Just call (520) 282-6523 to inquire about pricing, shipping and handling and so on. Checks may be sent to Light Technology, Box 1526, Sedona, Arizona 86339.

6

Angelic Medicines

Have you ever wished for divine healing for yourself or someone else? If you have $12, your wish can be fulfilled: $12 is the average price of a bottle of angelic medicine, and it is readily available to all who need it. Furthermore, angelic medicines require no prescription, have no unpleasant or harmful side effects whatever, and have a tendency to go straight to the hidden cause of each problem. Just what are these medicines? They are gem and flower elixirs, divine gifts from the Angelic Kingdom.

The techniques for making and using gem and flower elixirs were originally channeled from the Angels during the time of Lemuria and Atlantis, where many of us used them on a daily basis. If you are among those who used elixirs in ancient civilizations (including Egypt, Greece and China), you will find that they can also be of special benefit to you now, both personally and in your healing work.

In order to understand how gem and flower elixirs function, we must keep in mind the fact that everything that exists is a thought form. Here on the physical level we, our friends, our cars, our houses and all of the other things that we interact with physically are made up of mind energy vibrating so slowly that it is perceived as solid. This mind energy originates from the Divine Mind, which spins out the endless variety of thought forms that make up our world.

Disease is the result of the gradual deterioration of our individual thought forms as we struggle through a difficult series of incarnations here on Earth. Every negative experience that we go through distorts our self-image and the ways in which we perceive the world. Over the centuries these mistaken perceptions influence and change our individual thought form patterns, distancing us from our original mental, physical, emotional and spiritual perfection.

Flowers and gems are perfected thought forms that can be used as tuning forks to bring us back to our original patterns — to right thinking and right vibration. Flowers and gems are tended throughout their growth periods by members of the Angelic Kingdom; the beauty, color and the symmetry of flowers are the result of the Angels' precise thoughts, as are the luster, color and the geometric molecular lattices of crystals and gems. When flowers and gems are made into essences, sunlight transfers their perfected thought patterns into very pure water, which is then ingested as medicine.

One might think that a few drops of water that have simply had a flower or gem sitting in it for three or four hours couldn't have much healing power, but nothing could be further from the truth. Because water carries perfected thought energy right into the cells and DNA of our physical bodies, the impact on the physical form is enormous. In addition, since this energy is imprinted through pure light, it has a tremendous effect on the subtle (light) bodies where disease often begins. And lastly, because this energy is patterned by perfect thought, it also has the peculiar ability to reintroduce right thinking into body systems that have been damaged by wrong thinking. The end result is a sudden, clear understanding of a physical, mental, emotional or spiritual problem from an entirely different perspective. This dramatic change in viepoint frequently causes the disease or problem to fall away.

Flower and gem elixirs work especially well in cases where traditional medicine has failed. This is because traditional medicine tends to try to eliminate the symptoms of most problems rather than the underlying mental or emotional cause, whereas gem and flower elixirs focus on clearing up the wrong perceptions that are the root of the problem. When right thinking is reintroduced into the system, both cause and symptoms can often be released in a way that often seems nothing short of miraculous.

Fortunately, hundreds of gem and flower essences are available to us. Look for them in almost any metaphysical shop as well as many health food stores. The most well-known flower elixirs are the Bach Flower Remedies. Bach's famous Rescue Remedy is awesome: 2-4 drops of this mixture of five flowers can bring peace to those who are stressed, grieving, or even hysterical. It is wonderful before exams, job interviews or any other high-stress situation. The Rescue Remedy is also extremely useful to both healer and client before, during or after a healing session. Although the Bach remedies are more expensive than most, they are well worth the money and even a small bottle lasts a long time. There are 38 Bach remedies, all of which specialize in dealing with emotional problems. Bach puts out a flier that briefly describes the uses of each remedy, and there are several books on the subject. If you cannot find the remedies in a store near you, write or call Ellon Bach, 644 Merrick Road, Lynbrook, NY 11563, (516) 593-2206.

Pegasus Products makes literally hundreds of high-quality gem and flower elixirs, as well as the exotic Starlight Elixirs that were used in Lemurian and Atlantean spiritual initiations. If they are not available in your area you can write or call Pegasus Products, Inc., Box 228, Boulder, Colorado 80306, (800) 527-6104. Pegasus is associated with Gurudas, who has written (through two channels) several extremely useful books. These books may be ordered through your local metaphysical bookstore or through Pegasus; they are the "bibles" of the elixir healing profession. Everyone will benefit from *Gem Elixirs and Vibrational Healing, Vols. 1 and 2* (Volume 1 is the best), *Flower Essences and Vibrational Healing*, and *The Spiritual Properties of Herbs*, all by Gurudas. The elixir/essence books discuss the healing properties of hundreds of flowers and gems; give full instructions for making your own essences; and discuss how elixirs were used in Lemuria and Atlantis. The herb book focuses on spiritual changes brought about by herbs, flowers and trees and includes a fascinating discussion of sacred herbal practices in Lemuria, Atlantis, Egypt and China. Pegasus also has a catalog that briefly describes the uses of each of their best-selling elixirs.

It is likely that there are several other fine sources of elixirs available in your part of the country. A call to your local metaphysical shop will help you track them down.

A few tips: gem and flower elixirs integrate well with virtually any type of healing, especially when augmented by meditation. If you have several essences, you can mix them into many different specialized recipes for individual clients. Also, combining elixirs with aromatherapy (try the very pure floral scents) can be a marvelous, out-of-this-world experience.

Because elixirs push toxins out to the far edges of the auric field, regular soaking in mineral salt baths will remove the toxins and speed the healing process, as will consuming large amounts of distilled water with lemon. Aura Cacia makes a heavenly series of floral and herbal aromatherapy mineral baths as well as 52 essential floral and herbal oils. Write or call them at Box 399, Weaverville, California 96093, (800) 437-3301.

There are many strong forms of healing on our planet, but gem and flower essences are truly among the oldest and most effective. If you haven't yet experienced these exquisite elixirs from the Angelic Kingdom, you might consider doing yourself and your clients an enormous favor by trying them.

7

Healing with Elegance

he great angelic healing temples on the finer planes — as well as Earth's own ancient temples — all have one thing in common: healing methods that are both exquisite and impeccable. To simply attempt to heal is one thing, but to heal with style and elegance is the mark of an old soul who is strongly in touch with the spiritual dimensions. Such a healer pulls down an extraordinary energy, which she or he is then able to pass on to clients. Following are a few excellent techniques culled from several prominent healing temples that many of us have attended in past incarnations. You might consider trying them in your healing work; perhaps some of them will seem familiar

Anointing oils are a soothing and energizing way to begin a session, especially when used by healer and client. These oils are used on the chakras, generally the throat and third eye. For extra power, apply them in the shape of a cross, ankh and so on. Or try drawing a headband in oil across the forehead, to affect the right and left brain as well as the third eye. Those who heal with their hands will find it helpful to anoint their own third eye, heart and hand chakras (in the center of the palms and tips of the fingers) before a session. Crystal healers will find that anointing their crystals and gems will give the stones a luxurious and deeply sacred vibration. Massage therapists will find it useful to mix their own anointing massage oils. Some healers may prefer to use different oils on each chakra, providing the oils are mellow so their scents blend rather than clash. Anointing oils can be combined with deep meditation or placed on the third eye to increase any type of healer's ability to tune in during a healing session.

To make anointing oils, start with a base of pure almond oil and add a drop of essential oil such as rose, angelica, patchouli, sandalwood, lavender, frankincense, myrrh, ylang ylang, neroli or jasmine. High-quality essential oils are aromatic concentrates distilled from flowers, roots, leaves, barks and resins, all of which fall into the realm of angelic healing energies. Essential oils are extremely concentrated; one drop per 4 ounces of almond oil will be more than enough, so a little bottle will go a long way. If you are making a very small batch of oil, just dip the tip of a toothpick into the essential oil, then swirl the toothpick through the almond oil base — such a minute amount is generally quite sufficient. For extra zip, place a small quartz crystal or Herkimer diamond in the bottle to amplify the oil. Colored stones will create specialty oils; for example, green tourmaline is excellent for deep tissue work. Be sure to use a stone that is compatible with the chakras it will be used on. Whatever the final recipe, your anointing oil will keep best when refrigerated between uses. If you have no local source for essential oils, very high-quality materials may be purchased from Aura Cacia (see the preceding chapter for the address).

Fresh flowers can be placed above the client's crown chakra at the end of a difficult session — they will pour spiritual energy and perfected thought patterns into the auric field. Also, a healing room filled with a variety of potted plants is very relaxing and beneficial to the body, mind and spirit of both the client and healer.

A picture of a Spiritual Master is also a potent energy when placed above a client's crown chakra, as is a small geometric pattern of crystals and gemstones that harmonize with the crown energies (for example, amethyst, quartz, Herkimer, sugilite and so on).

A crystal pendulum spun clockwise above each chakra (starting at the base chakra) is a powerful and easy way to quickly open each chakra, balance it and fill it with light. To pull out negativity, twirl the pendulum counter-clockwise. However, after a counter-clockwise spin, always finish up with a clockwise motion so the chakra(s) will be open and ready to receive additional healing energy. If your pendulum is on a cord rather than a chain, another dynamic technique is to rotate the crystal counterclockwise by hand so the cord twists as tightly as possible; then hold the pendulum over a problem chakra and release the crystal. It will do a tight clockwise spin that sends an almost laserlike beam of light energy straight into the chakra. A twist and spin in the opposite direction will pull deep congestions out of a chakra. *Two spins per chakra is the maximum with this technique; don't overdo it, or it will damage delicate energies.* At the end of the session, be sure to clean the pendulum vibrationally.

Sound and light are the most potent healing forces in the universe, especially when used together. A well-known example of this combination used for cosmic creation is found in the Bible: In the beginning there was the Word . . . and the Word was "Let there be Light."

With regard to sound, classical music at a low volume is a profound tool that every healer can use. Very few people realize that the reason classical music has endured when most other music has faded into oblivion is because classical music reflects our genetic coding. The complex classical scores literally reproduce the encoded sequences found in human DNA. The musicians who wrote the music were simply channeling their own internal spiritual structure. Consequently, playing classical music during a healing session will help to splice and repair DNA damaged by past and current-life trauma. In light of this information, it would also seem logical that much of the channeled New Age music also carries genetic information from other dimensions as well as from races of extraterrestrial beings.

Light can easily be used in the form of colored light bulbs, and for a modest amount of money you can hang a small multiple-light fixture above a healing table, with a red bulb above the client's base chakra, yellow above the mid-chakras, green above the heart, blue around the head region and white above the crown.

The crystal light wands popular a few years back are another effective way to release a torrent of healing light into the chakras and subtle bodies. Basically these wands consist of a copper tube with a crystal mounted on one end and a small pen-sized flashlight in the other. Between the crystal and the flashlight is a small colored filter, which can easily be changed. The filters come in all the colors of the rainbow. In a darkened room, the wand's crystal will glow with the color of the filtered light, ranging from lemon yellow to deep magenta, indigo, cobalt blue, emerald green, lime, etc. Energize the first chakra with red light, the second with orange and so on, working your way up the chakras. Two minutes at each chakra will suffice. Ask your local crystal dealers if they have information on a source for these wands — they are difficult to find these days, but someone is probably still making them.

A light box is another way to bring superb light energy into a healing session or into your home or office. Small light boxes with colored filters for individual crystals are found in many metaphysical shops, but a larger model for crystal patterns can be made easily for under $10 using materials found around the house. A large light box is a real plus for any lightworker, since its energies can accomplish everything from keeping you warm during the winter, to taking a client on a spiritual journey in deep meditation.

To make a simple light box, find a medium-sized cardboard box or a plastic wastepaper basket, turn it upside down, cut a square out of the bottom and place a piece of glass over the hole (white glass from a stained-glass store is very nice, but regular glass will do). Put a small lamp with a 15-watt bulb (without the shade) inside the box/basket and turn it on. Next, place a geometric pattern of crystals or inexpensive tumbled stones on the glass and let the light disperse the energy pattern throughout the room.

After a minute or two you will feel a strong rush of energy flowing into your auric field. Because the energy from the light box is so powerful, it should be used for only about sixty minutes a day. Thirty minutes in the morning afternoon and evening will keep your house vibrant all day; five minutes at the start of each healing session will take your client deeper than ever before, especially if the light box is in the crown energy.

On a cold day a pink garnet pattern will circulate the energy through your auric field faster than usual and help you keep warm; blue stones will help cool down the auric field; amethyst will bring a spiritual energy into the room; and so on. Painting and decorating your light box with spiritual designs will affect not only the look but also the feel of the box. If you want to make a really terrific light box, start with a sturdy box such as an old stereo speaker or a wooden barrel. You can also buy large light boxes from photography shops and printer supply catalogues.

Finally, an atomizer filled with pennyroyal (an essential oil) will keep your healing room or house vibrationally clean. Spritz the room lightly before and after each session. The pennyroyal will remove any junk or trauma brought up by previous clients so the current client can start with a clean slate, impervious to other people's "stuff." Remember, cleanliness is truly next to godliness, especially in healing situations when a client's chakras are wide open and susceptible to whatever old energy might be lingering in the room.

8

Gathering Information
Before a Healing Session

Many healers — especially those in a metaphysical center like Sedona — are hampered in their work by the fact that frequently they see a client only one time and then the client leaves town. Because of the intimate nature of spiritual healing, it is therefore essential to immediately establish a strong, trusting relationship with each new client. If such a bond is not present, it is highly unlikely that the client will relax mentally and emotionally to the degree necessary to bring up and process deep trauma. It is also unlikely that the client will be able to get past defense mechanisms which cloak old anxieties, self-doubts and guilt. Furthermore, without a strong rapport with the client, the healer will generally not be able to pick up as much intuitive information about the source of a problem because the client will subconsciously be keeping the healer at arm's length, so to speak.

Unfortunately, getting to know someone takes time, which is generally not available to either the healer or the client. There are two ways around this. First, the healer can take about thirty minutes to meditate deeply on the client before he arrives and then discuss the findings with the client, hoping to loosen up the situation. At best, this is a short cut, but it can sometimes reveal astonishingly accurate information that will allow the healing work to progress at a much deeper level than is normal for a first session. A second and more reliable course of action involves typing a simple questionnaire, photocopying it, and filling it out with each client at the beginning of the first session.

Questionnaires have several advantages. They ask key questions that get right to the point and clue the healer in as to what type of trauma he/she is likely to encounter; they serve as a permanent record so the healer can better remember a one-time client from several years earlier; if a client comes several times, questionnaires can keep track of current developments in the client's life; and if the healer takes the time afterwards to add pertinent notes on the healing session, the questionnaire will chronicle not only the client's progress, setbacks, hopes, fears, problem areas and breakthroughs, but also the exact tools and methods employed by the healer during that particular session. Most healers have had the experience of thinking after a particularly difficult session, "Well, I'll never forget that client!" Then when the client turns up again a year later, the healer draws a total blank because of the intervening time and sessions with other people. With a competent questionnaire and notes on each session, this won't happen. Lastly, as you ask your client questions and discuss answers, you will be getting to know him/her and building an atmosphere of relaxation and trust.

What questions to ask? For starters, the obvious: date, name, address, phone number and age. It also helps to get the occupation, which can often provide vital clues to the person's specific problems. For example, people who encounter stress on the job will have a lot of unwinding to do before they can release deep problems. Doctors, nurses, psychiatrists, police officers and bartenders are a good example of people who pick up a lot of negative thought forms which need to be cleared out of the aura prior to a healing session.

Next, inquire as to the length of time the client has been involved in metaphysics. For a novice, it is helpful to explain what you will be doing, why, and how. Asking about a person's guides is also a good idea; it will tell you how tuned in they are and what type of guidance they are getting. A person with strong, clear inner guidance will be able to go deeper into the concentrated state of consciousness which facilitates clearing heavy trauma.

If your client knows about any of his/her past lives, this is also useful information for a healer to know, since many countries are known stress sites. For example, those who were incarnate in late Atlantean times often encountered bitter warfare, betrayal, murder, chaos and the like. People who incarnated with Christ frequently carry deep-seated guilt over not being able to stop the crucifixion. And those with Native American incarnations often reveal grief, despair and anger at the coming of the Europeans, the loss of family and land, and the destruction of the environment.

For those clients who are old-timers in metaphysics, it is helpful to know their main interests in the field; whether they are clairvoyant and/or clairaudient; and if they can visualize clearly. These things will often give you a handle on how to tackle a problem. For example, if a person is purely clairaudient, asking him/her to watch for pictorial information can be fruitless; try asking him to imagine that he is listening to a radio instead.

During a healing session some people will insist that the words or pictures that come to them are only their imagination. In such cases, it is vitally important to explain to them before the session that these impressions are usually their psychic senses sending them important symbolic information from the higher planes, and that you need to know about whatever they might see or hear during the session.

Another thing that is helpful to discuss is whether the client works with crystals, which are likely to have brought many problems from the DNA level up to the edge of consciousness where they will be waiting to be cleared.

Other things to find out include information on any existing physical, emotional and/or psychological difficulties or blocks and whether the client uses, or has ever used, tobacco, alcohol, drugs or prescription drugs. Of course, many people are reluctant to admit to drug use, but you can explain that drugs leave negative entities lodged in the chakras and, if they are removed, the healing will have a much stronger effect. If you work with crystals, pyramids, Power Tools or other high-energy devices, you should also find out if your client has hypertension because these tools can sometimes raise the blood pressure if they are used for long periods of time or in high-power combinations.

The next point is of *major importance:* when you ask about this, be sure to listen very carefully to the answer. The question is simple: Has the client ever had recurring nightmares? If so, ask him to describe them in detail. Most people will not remember anything or will produce nightmares they had as a child as the result of a misinterpretation (such as fear of clowns), a scary movie, or an upsetting children's book (the death of Bambi's mother, violent fairy tales, or cartoons and the like). These are generally isolated events that draw their impact from the fact that the personality was very young and unsteady. Unless the client attaches special significance to them, you needn't be overly concerned with this type of nightmare.

What is of concern to healers are recurring nightmares where the atmosphere is dark and depressing. These dreams often tie into some especially horrible past life trauma that has had such an impact on the soul that bits and pieces of the event surface over and over again in the sleep state. If a client has this type of nightmare it is likely to be the root of a major problem, and sometimes the trauma is lurking right beneath the surface just waiting to explode during a healing session. This can be frightening for both the client and the healer. So if your client has recurring nightmares, be forewarned that you are dealing with something extremely difficult. If you do past life regressions, try to find out the original circumstances, then trace the repercussions through the individual's incarnations between then and now. It will not be a pleasant session, but without this information it is almost impossible to clear the problem permanently.

Finally, it is a good idea to ask the client exactly what he/she would like to get out of the healing session. Many people are too shy or uncertain to mention what they are hoping for, so ask — and tailor your session accordingly.

As you can see, by the time you have finished with your questionnaire, you will know much more about your client than you would have without it, and your client will have had an opportunity to get to know and trust you as well. If, after the client has left, you follow up by adding notes about the session on the back of your questionnaire, you will find you have an invaluable resource not only for each particular client, but for many future clients who might have the same symptoms. A competent questionnaire — in combination with notes on the healing session itself — is the equivalent of a good healing text that can help you remember every client in detail, amass data, track progress, find chronic problems, make comparisons, and note similarities between clients. Above all, a good questionnaire allows you to be forewarned about the difficulties you are likely to encounter during a session.

9

Healing with Rainbows

A marvelous way to add pizzazz to a healing session is to use a small prism. A prism splits white light from the sun into the various healing rays, which will quickly energize a faded auric field and pour vibrant streams of radiant color into the physical and astral bodies.

Just before the session, healers can also use a prism to open their own crown, hand, and heart chakras. Opening the crown allows stronger, purer healing vibrations to flow down into your physical body. Opening the heart anchors the prismatic energies and sends them flooding into your hands. Opening the hand chakras allows the accumulated energies to pour out of your body in well-balanced, full-spectrum vibratory frequencies.

Begin by standing outside in the sunlight — or by a sunny window — and holding a prism about six inches above your crown. Be sure the prism is positioned so it throws its rainbows down toward the top of your head. Slowly breathe the rainbow light in through your crown chakra and concentrate on feeling the colors enter your body. Pull the colors in all the way down to your toes. After two minutes, move the prism to your heart chakra, turn it so the colored rays are splashed across your chest, and breathe the energy in through the heart for another two minutes. Last, hold the prism in your right hand and energize your left hand for two minutes, then change hands and energize your right hand for two minutes more. Focus the prism's rainbow into the center of your palms and pull the colors into your body as you inhale. Now proceed with your healing work. You should notice a big difference in your energy.

When the session is finished, take your client outside and direct the prism's light into her/his solar plexus chakra to energize the astral body. Then bring the prism to the navel for grounding, to the heart chakra to invigorate the physical body, and to the crown chakra to stimulate the flow of spiritual energies. If any particular part of the body is causing problems, give it a dose of light too. If your client is exceptionally low on physical energy or very depressed, hold your prism over his or her spleen, and the spleen chakra will automatically send the various colored rays to the parts of the body that need light the most.

Healers who work in the vortices will find that using a prism is an excellent way to purify your clients and tune their vibrations quickly and easily. Just be sure to keep your prism in a padded pouch to protect it from the rocks.

Rainbow light may also be used to charge water for a quick tonic after a healing session or for bathing wounds.

Excellent prisms may be ordered from Edmund Scientific, 101 East Gloucester Pike, Barrington, NJ 08007-1380. They have a wonderful catalog full of interesting healing tools — magnets, lasers, strobes, optical devices and so on. If you are in a hurry, call (609) 547-8880 and inquire about the optical glass Equilateral

Prisms ($4.45-$9.25), the Equilateral Triangle Class Prism ($7.95), or the Prism Discovery Set ($14.95), which has five sturdy acrylic prisms of various sizes.

Sedona residents can sometimes find acrylic prisms for under $5 at Mother Nature's in Tlaquepaque. The shop is in the Bell Tower Courtyard on the second floor.

10

Rose-Colored Glasses

An easy and inexpensive way to help chronically ill parts of the body maintain a proper vibration is to drink purified water from a colored glass. A solid-colored glass or goblet made of normal glass is preferable, since most glass contains quartz which will amplify the healing effect of the color. A solid-colored plastic glass is second best, although the vibration is very mild without the benefit of quartz acting as a booster. (Plastic glasses would be ideal for children or the elderly, where a gentle vibration is preferable.) Colored lead-crystal glasses or goblets should be avoided, as lead shuts down the chakras. Multicolors or patterns should also be avoided: stick with one pure, bold color.

It is best not to use your colored glass all of the time. A far more effective method is to use the glass for a week, use a clear glass for a week, go back to the colored glass for a week, then use the clear glass for a week and so on. Or you could use the colored and clear glasses on alternate days. The idea is to build a pulsating rhythm of colored light. A weekly rhythm would work more powerfully on the physical body, whereas a rhythm built on alternate days would tend to affect the astral body. Alternating colored and clear glasses hourly would most strongly effect the mental body. It is also possible to use more than one color, but they should be separated by the use of clear glass. For example, a week of green, a week of clear, a week of yellow, a week of clear, then back to green.

To help you determine which colors are best for you, the following attributes are culled from Dinshah, Gurudas and Choa Kok Sui.

Magenta: Opens the base chakra for women, which removes stress and releases past-life talents; balances and stimulates the aura, heart, circulatory system, kidneys and adrenals, emotions, and the reproductive system; a spiritual energy.

Red: Opens the base chakra for men and women, which removes stress and releases past-life talents; energizes the five senses; is an aphrodisiac; builds liver and blood; cleanses; energizes; can elevate blood pressure.

Orange: Opens the second chakra, which removes stress, anger, frustration, aggression, problems with self-system; promotes creativity; stabilizes emotions; energizes lungs, thyroid; builds bones, tissue; stimulates the stomach and the digestion; relieves cramps, muscle spasms.

Yellow: Opens the navel chakra, relieving stress and crippling diseases; stimulates neuromuscular system, tissue, lymphatic system, intestines, pancreas, stomach; energizes muscle; builds nerves; fights depression.

Lime: Opens the solar plexus chakra; alleviates psychosomatic and emotional problems; releases stress; integrates emotions; strengthens the connection with the astral body; also stimulates digestion, nutrition; acts as a laxative.

Green: Opens the heart chakra; balances the entire system, including the immune system; calms emotional extremes, brings harmony; aids the rebuilding of muscles and tissue; helps destroy germs and bacteria; cleanses.

Turquoise: Opens the throat chakra; encourages self-expression and spiritual abilities; stimulates the immune, endocrine and neurological systems; helps nutrition; skin.

Blue: Pineal stimulant; opens the third eye chakra for visualization, visions, insight, inspiration, intuition; relieves itching and irritation; is a mild sedative; builds vitality.

Indigo: Opens the higher forehead chakra above the third eye; stimulates parathyroid; depresses thyroid and respiratory function; controls abscesses; lessens secretions; arrests discharges and hemorrhages; promotes production of phagocytes, which destroy harmful microorganisms; reduces milk production; eases suffering; lessens excitement and overactivity; sedates.

Violet: Opens the crown chakra for spiritual fulfillment and perception of the divine forces; builds and stimulates the spleen; decreases muscular activity, including the heart; depresses lymphatics and pancreas; tranquilizes; promotes production of white blood cells.

Purple: Decreases sensitivity to pain; induces relaxation and sleep; lowers blood pressure, dilates blood vessels, reduces heart rate; decreases activity of kidneys and adrenals; lowers body temperature, controls fevers; depresses the emotions and reproductive system.

Rose: A marvelous color for the heart chakra in conjunction with green; balances and stimulates the emotions; sends divine love pouring into and out of the heart center; strengthens the heart and cardiovascular system. Rose is the color of prana (life force).

Hints

Twenty to thirty minutes of sunlight will amplify the vibration of the water. Water used in colored glasses should always be distilled or purified because it will have a marked cleansing effect at the cellular level and so should be free of minerals and microscopic debris. To amplify the cleansing effect, add a slice of fresh lemon.

As with most things, moderation and balance are the keys to effective color therapy. If you overdo it for, say, six months or a year, the constant vibratory input of one or two colors can throw the rest of your body out of tune. For maximum effect, if you are using the weekly method, alternate clear and colored water for four weeks, then stop using color for four weeks, then resume for four weeks. This gives you both a weekly and a monthly pulsation pattern that is much more powerful than a steady diet of color. If you are using a daily pulsation, do seven days' worth; skip for three weeks; then do another seven days and so on. If you are using an hourly pulsation, do one day every two weeks. The basic rule is this: a little well-timed color therapy is much more effective than a constant deluge.

If you doubt the difference a simple color can make, try putting distilled water in two glasses of different colors. Let the water sit in the sun for twenty minutes, then pour the water into two paper cups. Have several friends taste each cup: most people will notice a marked difference in the flavors of each cup, and some will be able to identify the color of the original glass by the taste or feel of the water.

Here's looking at you . . . through rose-colored glasses.

11

If You Don't Feel It, You Can't Heal It

There is a popular angelic saying on the finer planes that is given to healers about to (re)incarnate on Earth: "If you don't feel it, you can't heal it." The meaning behind the words is that a healer who has little or no experience of illness will generally not be able to heal on the deepest levels. This is because a great deal of empathy is required in order to be able to open the heart chakra enough to pull down multiple-frequency, highly specialized healing energies.

Have you ever had a problem that weighs heavily on you, shared the problem with a friend and gotten nothing but a laugh or a silly response? This happens when the other person has no similar circumstance in his/her own life to compare with your

problem. There is no connecting empathy, no depth of understanding or compassion. How much more satisfying it is to share
a problem with someone who knows precisely where you are
coming from and can sympathize with every small detail . . . yes?

Precisely the same thing is true of a healing experience. If the
healer understands the problem and can feel empathy with the
client, the healing session will be much, much more to the point,
the correct energies will flow freely, the healing will take place at
a significantly deeper level, and the results will last considerably
longer. If the healer has no empathy with the problem under
consideration, the healing session is likely to produce shallow
results at best.

Once a lovely man was driving through vortices at night, hit a
hairpin turn, missed it, rolled his truck and found himself trapped,
hanging upside down in the overturned vehicle. He stayed that
way for 18 hours in temperatures over 100 degrees after the sun
came up until someone happened by and rescued him. When a
local healer heard the story she said only, "Well, you must have
had something you needed to learn in order to have attracted this
lesson to yourself." Which is probably true enough, but . . . where
is the empathy? Sometimes a heartfelt, "Oh wow, what a miser-
able thing to have happen!" will go much, much further toward
helping the person mentally, emotionally and physically.

For reasons of empathy many very competent healers are
burdened by a great variety of illnesses, frequently chronic and/or
quite serious. People have a tendency to think, "Well, he can't be
much of a healer, look how sick he always is." Wrong! Each and
every illness or handicap we endure is a lesson, and that holds
especially true for healers. A good healer will experience a variety
of physical problems — and from time to time mental and emotional agonies — in almost every lifetime. Throughout his or her
series of earth incarnations a high-level healer will gain first-hand
knowledge of many types of chronic and deadly illness, as well as
loss or malformation of limbs, paralysis, anemia, malnutrition,

blindness, deafness, sexual abuse, physical violence, depression and the like.

And so the next time you see a healer who is leaning on a crutch, jaundiced, twenty-five pounds over- or underweight, sneezing, coughing, and wearing a large bandage . . . get his or her card! This could be a Superhealer, in the process of learning much more about the craft.

12

Hands That Heal

Imagine this scene: A healer is working with an ill, emotionally traumatized client. The client is lying on a table; the healer is working above him, moving her hands repeatedly through his auric field. As the healer works, she pulls negative entities out of the etheric webs covering his chakras; she smooths away the dark energies of anger, fear and frustration; she pulls white light down through her crown chakra and sends it pouring out through her hands into the client's physical and subtle bodies. Finally she places her hands on the client's feet and rebalances his energies by cycling them through her own body. When the session is over the client feels calm and invigorated; the healer is somewhat drained, but pleased with the way things went.

After the client leaves, the healer fixes herself a cup of tea and recharges for thirty minutes before dealing with her next client who, after many healing sessions, is on the verge of an emotional breakthrough. When the healer has finished with this second healing session she shuts the door to her healing room, walks into the kitchen and begins to prepare dinner for her family. After the meal is finished she does the dishes, plays a board game with her children and later tucks them into bed. Then she and her husband discuss their vacation plans, listen to music, watch a little TV, eat a late-night snack and eventually retire for the evening. This scene, with minor variations, is more or less the norm for many healers. Question: *What is drastically wrong with this picture?*

Imagine a second scene: The date is 1805. A doctor is working on a patient who has an ugly, festering wound. He cleans the infection as best he can, stitches the wound closed, cleans his hands on a towel and hurries across town to a house where a woman is giving birth. By the time the child is delivered it is past dinner time. The surgeon washes his hands in a bucket of cold water, dries them, puts on his coat, walks to his home and settles down to eat the meal his wife has prepared for him and his two children. After spending the evening chatting with friends, he and his wife go upstairs to bed. Question: *What is drastically wrong with this picture?*

Answer: *The exact same thing is wrong with both pictures.* From the viewpoint of 20th-century medicine, does it set your teeth on edge to imagine a doctor cleaning an infected wound with his bare hands and then delivering a baby, eating dinner, visiting with family and friends and going to bed without ever properly washing his hands? Can you imagine the consequences of such an action? Not only does the surgeon risk his own health, but also that of the newborn child, the child's mother, his wife, his own children and his friends.

Our fictitious 20th-century healer has done precisely the same thing. Just as the 19th-century doctor paid no heed to swarms of invisible germs, so also do many of our 20th-century healers pay little or no heed to equally dangerous astral entities and other conditions that are generally invisible on the physical dimension.

If you could have looked at the 19th-century surgeon's hands through a simple microscope, you would have seen swarms of deadly microbes spreading from his hands to the rest of his body and his clothes and onto every person, thing or bit of food he touched — for several days after the original surgery.

If you could watch the 20th-century healer from the astral plane, you would see swarms of leechlike negative thought elementals being forced out of the client's aura and immediately taking up lodging in the healer's auric field. Each time she passes her fingers through the client's aura as she cleans it, her hands pick up what looks like a thick coating of odiferous mud. Layer after layer of this unpleasant, lower-astral material accumulates over her hands, arms and body during a normal healing session. As she pours light out to the client through her own auric field, the debris settles deeper into her own aura. When she drinks her tea between clients, she takes this material inside her body. When she works with her next client, she spreads a large amount of the decayed astral material throughout the client's auric field and chakra system. As she cooks dinner she mixes astral slime into her family's meal. During the course of the evening she spreads astral catastrophe throughout her house, all over her children and husband, and then carries it into bed with her. And these unpleasant conditions are likely to continue in her house for several days after the original healing work.

Feeling queasy? Indeed! And yet we all do this to a greater or lesser degree. Even those who are not professional healers have done it: perhaps it is an action as simple as massaging a friend's back and shoulders during a hard day and then going back to your own tasks. The next time you eat a sandwich or a piece of fruit or drink a glass of water, you may be bringing noxious astral material from your friend's auric field into your mouth and body via your hands.

What to do? If possible, begin by stepping outside as soon as each client leaves and shaking your hands and arms violently, visualizing that you are flicking off heavy spatters of mudlike astral accumulations. Then wash your hands and arms thoroughly *all the way up to your elbows* in preparation for your next client. Finish up by going outside again and visualizing a beam of intense white light pouring down over your crown chakra like water, washing away any debris and negative elementals that might be clinging to the rest of your body.

Any crystals and healing tools used during a session must also be cleaned between clients: the popular Microcrystal Cards (sold at many metaphysical shops for $7-$10) are fast and easy for this type of cleaning. Simply put your tools/crystals on the cards for 15 minutes and they will be thoroughly cleaned vibrationally. (If your local shops do not carry Microcrystal cards, call the Crystal Castle in Sedona at (520) 282-5910, or Crystal Magic at (520) 282-1622.)

Smudging your healing room with incense between clients is also an excellent idea — the high vibrations produced by burning incense will dissolve sloughed-off astral material that accumulates around the healing area and on your healing table.

While you are actually working on a client, a bucket of salt water placed nearby will absorb and neutralize negative astral energies as they are released; flicking your fingers frequently above this bucket will help keep your hands and arms relatively clean.

Finally, when your healing day is finished, a hot shower is mandatory before you walk repeatedly through your house, prepare or eat a meal, or spend time with family and friends etc. If you can't wash your hair at the end of every day, then use a shower cap and let the water pour through your crown chakra energy for several minutes. If your clients have had more trauma than usual, after your shower fill the tub with hot water, add some bath salts or herbs to neutralize your auric field, and then soak your whole body for fifteen to twenty minutes. If the day has been extremely difficult in terms of your clients' emotional trauma and/or physical illness, rinse off in the shower a second time after your bath. Next, treating yourself to a glass of distilled water with a little lemon juice in it will finish the cleansing and realign your electromagnetic field. And if you feel that any of your home's living spaces have been contaminated, clean them immediately with incense or a smudge stick.

It's true that following these procedures can be a hassle during and after a long day, but it's also true that you, your clients, your home, your family and your friends will be happier and much, much healthier — physically, emotionally and spiritually — as a result of these simple precautions. Let's bring our healing work out of the Dark Ages!

13

Healing with the Dolphins

Since the days of Atlantis, dolphins have shared their healing powers with mankind. These marvelous, highly evolved beings specialize in helping humans heal battered minds and emotions, with emphasis on trauma brought over from past lives. Any healer can call on the dolphins during a healing session, and the dolphins will quickly respond.

Perhaps you remember one of the Dolphin Temples in ancient Atlantis. The one I remember was a square white structure similar to Greek temples, built of white stone, with many graceful columns. This particular building sat on a bluff overlooking a serene turquoise bay. There was a sandy, tree-lined path leading up to the temple, and in front of the building was a fountain spraying a mist of water that picked up rainbow hues from the sun. Projected into this colorful mist were holograms of leaping dolphins. As people walked through the door of the temple, a huge emerald-green ocean wave — another hologram — washed over them and cleansed their auric field.

The Dolphin Temples were for mental and emotional disorders. If you are interested in this type of healing, it is possible that you had a connection with these temples and with their dolphin allies. The following message regarding their temples and healing work recently came to me in a dolphin meditation.

"We are a nation of Star Children, as are many of you. We come to help bring peace and harmony to a world that is filled with strife and discord. Our mission is a gentle one, misunderstood by many. We have come to bring intelligence to this world so our light may help eradicate the darkness that surrounds the planet and fills the oceans, stifling her life forms.

"It is now time to make a conscious link between your species and ours; it is time for many of us to begin working together in order to intelligently shape the tides of world events.

"Long ago when our temples stood high on Atlantean hills, dolphins and man communicated with one another at a level that has not been achieved since. We had much to offer your kind and you had much to offer us, so we joined our thoughts, our efforts and our beings to try to accomplish that which had never before been attempted on this planet. And we succeeded! Our temples were places of cleansing, light and self-knowledge. They were places where those who were broken in spirit could come to reintegrate all the facets of their being.

"Those who had lost their mental balance were invited to swim in the ocean with us in order to regain the unity of their primordial selves, when all life forms swam in an undifferentiated sea of pure energy. We worked with these damaged beings; we sent our sonic waves into their auric fields and bounced healing sound off their physical and subtle bodies, thereby tuning and reharmonizing them. The sea washed away the darkness that filled them and brought them a new sense of peace, balance and belonging. We swam with many such people, and they were as our children. They brought us much joy, and we returned that joy to them.

"We swam with youngsters who had no mothers; we swam with those who had been damaged by war; we swam with those who had taken the lives of their own kind; we swam with those who were encased in the darkness of despair; we swam with those who could not distinguish reality from that which was not real.

"In our ocean environment many released their misery, many slowly began to regain their sense of balance and their perspective, many began to smile and then to laugh. Many were rebirthed in this great ocean of ours, which is truly the mother of us all.

"Now we would like to work with you again in this way. We would also like to return the sea to her former purity so that once again she may perform this act of motherhood, of rebirthing those of you and those of us who are bearing the stress of these new times.

"The dolphins in captivity find it difficult to survive direct contact with people, for they lack the freedom of the ocean which connects them with their brothers and with their spiritual strength. They are somewhat isolated and lonely in many ways, although they try to withstand these pressures. When those of your kind who are under stress swim with them, rather than having the ocean cleanse the negative energies, the imbalance and stress are sloughed off onto the captive dolphins, filling their swimming space and drastically shortening their lifespan.

"So for now we ask you to come to us primarily through meditation, to psychically cast your nets out into the sea and haul in a harvest of ideas. Experience us not only through words — for words are limiting, and what we have to offer is beyond limits — but come and know us through deep meditation so you can truly relate to our lives and our unique perspective. Share yourselves with us as you look upon the world in a way that you have never seen before. Gain a different point of view and take that knowledge back to your people. Share with them all that you learn, all that you and we jointly hope to be — for life is everlasting, and every moment is what we make of it.

"Together we can change this earthly life into something grand, something splendid, something that will resonate with balance and energy now and throughout all of the ages to come.

"We invite you to swim with us!"

Connecting with the Dolphins

The following technique is given by the dolphins; it is very simple and effective. If possible, listen to a dolphin tape as you meditate. Sit quietly and focus your thoughts.

Begin to watch for a golden triangle in the center of the blue ocean of your mind. When you see it clearly, visualize yourself diving down deeper and deeper, until you come to this triangle and swim through it. Threading your consciousness through the triangle activates the pituitary gland and connects it with the kundalini energy.

As you swim through the triangle, one or more dolphins will generally appear — just relax and go with the flow. The dolphins may begin by giving you channeled healing information, or they may swim with you, or take you somewhere, depending on the situation.

If you get no results on your first attempt, try energizing your third eye with a quartz crystal or a Power Tool. Then use the pyramid meditation technique that is given in the meditation section of this book: from the top of your pyramid, try the triangle technique again.

14

The Subtle Bodies:
What They Are and
How They Work

N ew Age healers usually concern themselves with the astral body as well as the physical because they attempt to treat the whole person. However, in actuality, the physical and astral bodies add up to only one-third of the total being. And if you consider the fact that the physical and astral bodies are the most limited vehicles, the figure drops to much less than that.

We actually have so many bodies that it is difficult to keep track of them. This month let's discuss the soul's descent into matter and find out how we manifested on this little blue planet in the first place, and why.

The Seven Planes of Existence

In the elegant scheme of creation there are seven enormous planes of existence, each vibrating at a different rate. The first plane, which has the highest vibration, is occupied by the Godhead. From this unfathomable center the wave of creation bursts forth, flowing outward to form the second great plane. Vibrating at a slightly lower pitch, this second plane adjacent to the Godhead is the original, true home of your soul. It is a place of limitless light and glory where the soul experiences perfect, inexpressible bliss.

Onward and outward from the second plane the wave of creation continues, forming the third great vibratory plane, then the fourth, fifth, sixth and seventh planes. With each succeeding plane the vibration lowers, becoming more and more dense, until the seventh plane is formed of energy vibrating so slowly that it solidifies to form physical matter. This is where our universe is situated, on the seventh plane of creation.

When a soul decides to visit the physical plane for the purpose of knowledge, growth, service and adventure, it does so by stepping part of its energy down through each of the vibratory levels until it reaches the seventh plane. As it passes through the great layers of creation on its downward journey, it forms a body out of the material of each plane so it will have vehicles through which it can explore and learn at every level simultaneously.

The entity that is you, therefore, is composed of your physical body here on the difficult seventh plane. The physical body connects to your astral body operating on the sixth plane. The astral body is linked to a mental body working on the fifth plane, and from there the chain continues to the causal body on the fourth plane, the buddhic body on the third plane and the pure soul itself dwelling on the nirvanic second plane, adjacent to the Godhead (which occupies the first plane).

Very highly advanced metaphysicians perceive the scheme of

the vibratory planes slightly differently, as this explanation is somewhat simplified. But it will give you a general idea of the basic order of things without becoming unduly entangled in nuances that do not concern us here. The most notable omission in the above summary is the etheric body, which is a sort of buffer zone between the physical and astral bodies. Since it is not a separate vehicle of higher consciousness, it will suffice to mention it here in passing and leave it at that.

Raising Vibrations

The higher the vibratory plane, the wider the range of possibilities that become available to the body existing on that level. As the vibrations rise, there is a corresponding expansion of dimensions, so while our physical bodies are limited to three dimensions, our astral forms enjoy the freedom of four dimensions, our mental bodies function in five dimensions and so on. This is why metaphysical adventures and spiritual insights from meditation into the higher dimensions are so difficult to express in terms of our narrow three-dimensional existence. They simply must be experienced in order to be comprehended.

It should be emphasized that the seven great planes of creation are not so much places as states of vibration. For example, ice consists of hydrogen and oxygen atoms vibrating so slowly that they take on solid form. Raise the vibrations of the ice by heating it, and it turns to water. Heat it some more, and as the vibrations continue to rise the water changes into visible steam. With further heating the steam soon becomes invisible vapor in the air. The original hydrogen and oxygen atoms do not necessarily have to change their location in order to make the transition from solid ice to indiscernible vapor — they merely have to raise their vibrations.

Our physical bodies are similar to the ice, vibrating so slowly as to be solid in form. Our astral bodies, vibrating more rapidly, are more fluid, like water. Our mental bodies are on the order of

steam, and our higher subtle bodies, as well as our souls themselves, are oscillating at such keen rates that we cannot even
remotely detect them with our physical senses or even our astral
senses. They are the equivalent of vapor and far beyond. It is an
imperfect illustration, but the concept is there and you can see that
location has little or nothing to do with the various planes. Instead, the whole thing hinges solely on rates of vibration; thus
entire vast planes may actually interpenetrate one another and
occur simultaneously, so long as their vibratory rates are different.

This means you don't really have to travel anywhere in order
to get to the astral plane, the mental plane or beyond. You simply
have to raise your vibrations enough to give you access to your
astral body, your mental body or whichever vehicle interests you.
Many people who are evolving with this planet have higher bodies
that are dormant. These bodies exist on the higher planes, but in a
comatose, embryonic state. Most lightworkers, on the other hand,
have fully developed bodies on the finer planes, and many will
find that it is possible to use their higher vehicles to gather information. Consequently, when healing other lightworkers, it is well
to remember that each of these active subtle bodies has an unusually direct impact on the physical body and vice versa because
they all overlap and interconnect, like the links of a chain.

The connecting points for the various subtle bodies are located
in the physical brain and spinal column at sites corresponding to
the major nerve junctures. Vital energy flows through these centers into the physical body from each of your finer bodies, so you
exist not only on physical energy, but your body also requires a
certain amount of astral, mental, causal, buddhic and nirvanic
energies as well.

The cerebrospinal centers that channel this inflowing energy
from the higher planes into the physical form resemble whirlpools
of incoming light/energy. Therefore, they are called chakras, from
the Sanskrit word for wheels. We count seven or sometimes eight
major chakras — some people count thirteen — but there are also

hundreds of minor chakras all over the surface of the body, which we know as the acupuncture points. These minor chakras are formed by criss-crosses in the energy lines emanating from the major chakras. The lines of energy that link the minor chakras are called *meridians*. As you might have already guessed from the description, this vast system of chakras and meridians corresponds very nicely with the Earth's vast network of vortices and ley lines. The terminology is different, but the appearance and function of the energy flow are similar.

Just as your chakras bring energy and information to your physical body from your subtle bodies dwelling on higher levels, so the Earth's vortices bring energy and information to the physical globe from her vehicles on the finer planes. And just as the Earth's massive energy fields are balanced through her system of vortices and ley lines, so your physical and nonphysical energies are balanced through your arrangement of chakras and meridians. When you balance and align your chakras in a vortex area such as Sedona, you are aligning all of your vehicles on every plane with all of the Earth's vehicles on every plane. This powerful synchronization is what might be termed a grand alignment, which is why people have such awesome experiences in vortices.

With all of the above in mind, it can easily be seen that when you do chakra work, you are in fact affecting the *whole* person in the fullest sense of the word, all the way up to the soul level. This is also why crystals, Power Tools and other New Age products generate such tremendous results when they are placed on the chakras.

And so it becomes more and more apparent that if you truly wish to heal on all possible levels, the answer to achieving your goal is — chakra power!

15

Understanding the Chakras

In the last chapter we discussed the soul's descent into matter, the formation of the subtle bodies, and the way in which chakras act as conduits for energy flowing down from the subtle bodies on the finer planes. Now let's take a closer look at the individual chakras.

States of healing, as well as deep states of superconsciousness, are achieved by working through the chakra system in order to access the subtle bodies. Authorities differ as to the exact number, location and color scheme of the chakras. This is due primarily to different body types and the degree and direction of each individual soul's evolution. For example, there is much controversy over whether the third chakra is located at the navel or the solar plexus. Both locations are correct: people who have incarnated extensively in our Western civilizations will tend to focus energy in the navel chakra, while individuals who have incarnated time after time in Eastern civilizations will focus energy in the solar plexus. When in doubt, balance both chakras.

The chakra system presented here is simple and effective for everyone, since it includes both navel and solar plexus chakras. We will discuss thirteen chakras that run in a fairly straight line from the groin to the top of the head and somewhat beyond.

Seen from the side, the chakras look like whirling funnels of colored light. The narrow ends of the funnels are attached to the spinal column, pass from the back of the body through to the front, and widen out several inches beyond the front of the body.

Seen from the front, the chakras look like flowers with opened petals, or ornate wheels with many spokes. These effects are due to the energy lines that radiate from the center of each chakra. The number of petals or spokes that manifest depends on the frequency of the energy flowing through each center. The lower earth frequency of the base chakra manifests only four petals, while the much higher spiritual frequency of the crown chakra manifests a thousand petals of cascading light.

Because the spinal energies raise their frequency as they flow upward, there is also a rainbow effect to the colors of the chakra system, ranging from infrared at the groin to ultraviolet and bright gold around the top of the head.

All in all, the living light of the chakra system is a beautiful sight to behold as it pulsates with brilliantly-hued energy flowing in from all the different planes of creation. Normally, this energy field (the aura) spreads out to a distance of about eighteen inches from the physical body. However, when a person begins to evolve spiritually, pulling more and more high-frequency energy down from the finer planes into the physical body, the colors of the chakras purify into a dazzling resplendency that defies description as the auric field grows larger and larger. Just imagine: the Masters say the Buddha's aura had a radius of three miles!

It is well worth our while to take a brief look at each center separately, because if you understand your chakras you will better understand yourself.

The first, or base, chakra grounds your soul's energy onto the physical plane. This chakra opens in the lower pubic region from whence it connects back to the tip of the spine (coccyx). It vibrates at the deep red end of the spectrum, sometimes displaying a violet tinge. For men this is the sexual center. The first chakra stores stress and pollution; when its energy is balanced, tension is released. A well-tuned base chakra leads to emotional stability and a feeling of being focused, centered and grounded. The colors red and black respectively open and ground this earth-oriented chakra. When the first chakra is overactive (as in the case of sexual obsession), green closes it.

The second chakra is midway between the first chakra and the navel: it is a beautiful, vibrant orange color. Closely connected with creativity and motherhood, this is the sexual center for women. Stress, anger and sexual repression result when this chakra is out of adjustment. Balancing the second chakra leads to increased creativity, integrated emotions and greater success in intimate relationships. Orange opens this center; blue closes it.

The navel center works in conjunction with the solar plexus and displays a bright yellow glow. Psychosomatic and emotional problems, grief, depression and stress can result from an imbalance of this energy. A balanced navel chakra heightens sensitivity and intuition. Yellow opens the navel center; violet closes it.

The solar plexus chakra is as bright as the noonday sun, shining with a brilliant golden-white light. This complex chakra is the juncture of the lower chakras — the earth-oriented centers — and the higher spiritual centers. The astral body connects to the physical body through the solar plexus chakra. The astral vehicle is sometimes referred to as the emotional body because it is the seat of our emotions. This is why inner turmoil causes a tight feeling in the region of the solar plexus, because negative emotions flow through that chakra directly into the astral body, resulting in tension at the connecting point. If you wish to clear emotional problems, this is the chakra on which to focus. Trauma from past lives and old karma also leave their residue in the solar plexus energy, and this usually must be dissipated before progress is possible on higher levels. A harmonious solar plexus brings emotional serenity, physical well-being and an increasing ability to use the astral body during sleep. Clear white light and gold open the solar plexus; since white light is composed of all the colors, no pure color closes it.

The heart chakra is green, although a happy, mellow heart center throws out every color of the rainbow in clear, delicate shades. Imbalance in the heart energy leads to circulatory problems, deficiencies of the immune system and emotional extremes. This is the major balancing center for the physical and subtle bodies; just as the physical heart pumps blood to all parts of the body, so the heart chakra pulsates energy throughout the auric field. In addition, the astral body has a strong influence on the heart center, as does the soul itself. An open, loving, divinely-connected heart chakra such as that of Christ looks like a constantly changing kaleidoscope of complex patterns and exquisite colors. Many pure colors open the heart; green is the primary color, but gold, pink and violet are also highly desirable.

The throat chakra is light blue in color. This chakra controls astral hearing (clairaudience) and many nonvisual types of channeling, as well as the ability to express oneself clearly and effectively. Problems with the throat energy impact the speech centers and the immune system, and the inability to express oneself can lead to illness resulting from suppressed emotions. Light blue opens the throat; orange closes it.

The third-eye chakra is so ubiquitous that it even appears on our one-dollar bill, and just about every culture has knowledge of it. Actually, there are two centers of psychic vision, one low on the forehead and one higher up. It is both of these centers working together that gives your inner vision clarity and focus, just as your two physical eyes working together give physical depth perception. The energy of the lower third-eye center vibrates at a deep cobalt-blue frequency; the higher fourth-eye center manifests indigo blue. An imbalance in either center causes hallucinations and an inability to distinguish fantasy from reality. Balanced psychic centers, however, bring valuable gifts: intuitive understanding, spiritual inspiration, the ability to visualize clearly, and visions of the finer planes and of the Divine Mind. Since the mental body connects to the physical brain via the third and fourth eye centers, it is through these chakras that access is gained to the fifth dimension. Cobalt blue and indigo open the third and fourth eyes respectively; red and yellow close them.

The crown chakra has as its colors violet and lavender. It is through this vital center that divine forces nourish the physical being. Because of the divine energy flow, there is no negativity associated with the crown chakra. Through the soft skin over the crown the spirit enters the body of the child in the womb; often through this same doorway the life force retreats upon the death of the physical body. A fully opened crown chakra radiates divine Light in the thousand-petaled lotus shape referred to in the Eastern scriptures. When this center is balanced, connection with the Divine is felt. Violet and lavender open the crown; no color closes it.

The five chakras above the crown are nonphysical centers that connect with the highest subtle bodies. We will not deal with them in detail, as it will suffice to say that pink, silver, and deep gold are the essential colors here, and there are also other colors that go beyond the physical spectrum. The gold nimbus seen in portraits of Christ and the great Masters refers to this energy.

Your Doorways to Limitless, Multidimensional Possibilities

Since the energy of each chakra maintains the body organs in its vicinity, a chakra system that is properly cleaned, balanced and aligned is a ticket to improved physical well-being. Because the higher chakras connect to the subtle bodies, they are also windows that look out on glorious, divine landscapes. Through these windows you can explore other times, other places, other worlds, other dimensions and other forms of being. Through them also you can contact the Divine Mind and the Holy Masters, which marks the beginning of deep spiritual fulfillment.

Down through the chakra system sweeps the multidimensional energy that sustains the physical body; up through the chakra system flows the information gathered from this plane on its way to the soul itself. Needless to say, it behooves us all to keep this vital energy network functioning as perfectly as possible.

For a brilliant discussion of the chakras, see Gurudas' *Gem Elixirs and Vibrational Healing, Vol. 1.* Also highly recommended is Leadbeater's *The Chakras*, which includes colored pictures of each chakra.

The Death Experience:
Making the Big Transition

As healers, sooner or later we are all bound to have clients who are in the terminal stages of illness. Unfortunately, on this planet death is considered to be a sad, terrible thing in spite of the fact that every major religion teaches the concept of life after death. The simple truth is, life on this difficult, dense physical dimension is as dead as we get — it is only when we leave the body permanently that our greater lives begin.

You can help terminally ill clients greatly by reminding them of this simple fact. And once their fear has been alleviated, they just might not turn out to be terminal after all. This is because the very diagnosis of cancer, AIDS or any other fatal illness sets up such an overwhelming fear mechanism that the immune system and the body's other fighting defenses literally shut down in terror, which does indeed lead to death. It goes like this: tell someone convincingly that he is going to die and chances are good that he will do it. But if you point out that death is merely a graduation to a higher, infinitely more pleasant phase of existence, the fear is alleviated, the body strengthens and inner balance has a chance of being restored. Or, should this truly be his time to go, at least he can do so in a calm, peaceful, relaxed state of mind.

What Is Death?

The *Bhagavad-Gita* has this to say about death:

Never the spirit was born,
The spirit shall cease to be never.
Never was a time it was not:
End and beginning are but dreams.
Birthless and deathless and changeless remaineth the spirit for-
ever.
Death hath not changed it at all, dead though the house of it
seems.
It is as when one lays his worn out robes away
And, taking new ones, says, "These will I wear today!"
So lightly puts away the spirit its garb of flesh,
And passes to inherit a residence afresh.

How many times do you suppose you have taken off your clothes at the end of a weary day without giving it a thought? That's probably just about how many times you have shed your physical form on this planet. It need be no more complex or tragic than that, except when it's compounded by fear of the unknown.

Reflect on how grueling this life is. Consider that during an average lifetime pain, illness, emotional insecurity, mental vacillation and unhappy relationships are standard fare, and for many, fire, flood, pestilence, starvation, abandonment, drugs, alcohol, handicaps, physical violence, insanity, war, rape and so on are liable to be present in varying degrees while we learn the lessons offered on this plane. Being freed from all these states of uncertainty would be like being released from a dungeon — so what's to fear or mourn? At worst it's a momentary separation from friends and family. At best it's a blessed release from life's agonies.

If you or a loved one were going on an extended vacation, you would probably begin making your plans well in advance. So why not help prepare yourself and others for the much greater trip back to the astral plane? Understanding exactly what happens at death can give you such preparation.

The Death Experience

As the soul readies itself to slip away from its cumbersome outer casing, it begins to methodically withdraw its energy from the physical feet, legs, torso, hands, arms and so on, and transfer this energy to the astral body. The person making the transition begins to feel somewhat numbed, similar to the sensation experienced when a limb goes to sleep. At the same time the physical senses begin to dull also — sight, touch, taste, smell and hearing start to fade as the soul gathers itself in. But, while the physical senses diminish, the astral psychic senses often expand and become more acute. Dying persons frequently become conscious of sights and sounds in distant places or are aware of the presence of deceased loved ones.

After a while the astral body slowly begins to rise, disengaging from the physical form. Depending on the circumstances and the soul's spiritual development, different chakras serve as the exit. Those who have witnessed the samadhi of great Masters report hearing a popping sound as the soul exits straight up through the crown chakra. Other exits include the third eye chakra (the light-at-the-end-of-the-tunnel experience), the heart chakra, and the solar plexus.

As the astral body is released, it appears as a bluish, smoky haze that gradually solidifies and re-forms into a semblance of the physical body. It then floats face down directly above its physical counterpart, where it hovers for a last look, to piece together exactly what is happening and to try to comfort loved ones who might be present.

Just as in physical birth, eventually the astral cord (similar to the umbilicus) connecting the soul to the physical form snaps, the astral light is extinguished around the physical body, and the astral body begins to float away on the astral currents. Consciousness is generally dreamlike and hazy as the soul begins its transition. However, at this time many people have the presence of mind — or the sheer determination — to project their astral forms to absent loved ones as a sort of farewell.

On the other hand, if death occurs suddenly and/or violently, the person might not fully understand that he or she is actually dead. Under these circumstances the astral body is disconnected from the physical form so quickly that the soul simply doesn't realize what has happened. If you meditate on this, each of you will probably remember past lives when this has occured. I was machine-gunned to death with a group of people in a concentration camp during my last incarnation, and as I fell I remember thinking that I must be cleverly pretending to be hit, because I felt no pain whatsoever. I lay there while the guards kicked us over to be sure we were dead, and much to my amazement they seemed to believe that I was. Minutes later my astral body lifted up into the air and as I looked down I realized that my physical body was indeed decimated and that I must truly be dead. Sure enough, I was! The only painful thing about the experience was the fear we all felt beforehand when we were ominously herded outside the camp.

At any rate, once the transition has been made, you are not a different person at all: you are exactly who you were on the physical plane, only without the dense physical form. You still have the same mind, virtues, faults, likes and dislikes as before;

only your surroundings have changed. It's like moving from Minneapolis to Hawaii — the scenery is more exotic, you wear lighter clothing, but . . . it's still you.

A common problem at this stage is that the astral body contains seven different types of astral material, and after disengaging from the physical body these elements tend to rearrange themselves into a series of shells, with the densest, coarsest layers on the outside. This shelling holds the soul at the lower astral subplanes until the outermost layer disintegrates, at which point the soul rises to the next level, where it remains until the second shell disintegrates. Gradually the soul works its way up through the seven astral subplanes, shedding material from each level as it goes, until it has reached the highest subplane. (It should be emphasized that this is not an upward movement through space, but through vibratory realms.) This slow, tedious rearranging can be avoided by using your will power to visualize that the astral particles which comprise your astral body are kept in an intermingled state, with a strong white Light flowing through your entire astral form. Visualize it like the darting snow you get on your TV set when the channel is out.

Another thing that interferes with the soul's upward rise is the reluctance of some souls to leave the physical world. Whether they are attached to loved ones or to vices such as drugs and alcohol, such people literally draw an etheric shell around themselves, which serves only to cut them off from both the physical and astral worlds. There are always astral helpers to aid in transitions, but if a person has shelled herself or himself, sometimes even the astral helpers cannot get through until the shell disintegrates. Ghostly hauntings are generally the work of these obsessed earthbound souls. The light-filled prayers and good wishes of unselfish loved ones can greatly help speed such souls on their way and disintegrate their imprisoning shells.

The Soul Slumber

Just as the physical body requires rest after a long day, so the astral body requires a period of sleep and recuperation after a lifetime tied to the heavy physical plane. Thus shortly after death the soul begins to slip into a deep sleep in order to rest and prepare for life on the astral plane — this is similar to the time the soul spends in the mother's womb as it prepares for its physical incarnation.

The soul's deep sleep takes place on a vibratory plane which is sacred and totally safe, for none may enter there except Ascended Masters. During its slumber the soul reviews its recent lifetime: it sees every detail of its past existence, analyzes its actions, traces the ramifications of each act, determines where it failed and where it succeeded, and lays plans for future incarnations. While this is happening the soul is also discarding many of the less noble aspects of its nature, burning them away as it takes stock of its lessons. There is no judgment of the soul except that which the soul passes on itself during this time of self-evaluation.

Awakening

Eventually the soul begins to slowly awaken as it slips away from the lower energies that it has discarded: at this point it truly opens its eyes to the beauties of the spectacular astral worlds. Now the soul is ready for some high adventure! Next month we will discuss the soul's sojourn on the astral plane, including the scenery, the inhabitants, and what astral life is like, as well as the soul's eventual decision to either reincarnate on Earth again or rise to the next vibratory level, ending its series of physical incarnations altogether.

17

Resurrection on
the Astral Plane

When we earth-weary souls begin to come out of our deep astral sleep, little do we imagine the glorious life that awaits us. As we open our astral eyes we are surrounded with exquisite landscapes formed of chasms of multicolored light: brilliantly shining rainbow skies with soft, pearly clouds; majestic mountains glowing in mesmerizing blends of greens, purples and blues; emerald meadows dressed in a profusion of shimmering, gem-colored wildflowers; graceful, radiant trees with leaves that flash in the gentle breeze; oceans, lakes, ponds, rivers and streams alive with sparkling, opalescent waters. Next we notice the pleasant warmth of sunshine; the sweet, spicy, soul-stirring scents of flowers and trees; the poignant melodies of songbirds. Every astral object glows with life force — and suddenly our whole existence is one with the Light. Coming joyously toward us are deeply cherished loved ones whom we have not seen for a very long time. Such are the pleasures that await our souls after the trials and tribulations of Earth.

If you are clairaudient, you will find an astral scene like this wonderfully described in Beethoven's Sixth (Pastoral) Symphony: Listen with earphones if you can, breathe deeply and put yourself into the music. You will sense the astral sky, meadow, wildflowers, trees and birds. As the symphony progresses you will experience an afternoon thunderstorm and literally feel the astral sun reappear when the storm is over. It is a wonderful piece of channeled astral music!

If you are clairvoyant, see if your library has a book on Maxfield Parrish's paintings: They too describe the astral plane, focusing on the delicious play of astral light on the landscape. These superb paintings are also channeled and should jog some of your own memories of the astral realms. Also, if you would like to experience a few of the many wondrous astral colors, try to attend a good laser light show.

Finding Your Niche

The vast astral plane has many, many subplanes, each with its own scenery formed by the collective thought forms of the people who reside there. Every ascending soul is automatically drawn to the subplane that best suits it in terms of vibration, scenery, belief systems, like-minded souls, and developmental opportunities. So a Native American from Earth's 19th century might find himself in a beautiful natural setting with abundant herds of animals, plenty of fruit and vegetables ripe for the gathering, and dwellings similar to what the soul experienced on Earth. A Christian who takes the Bible literally might find himself in a beautiful city with pearly gates and streets paved with gold. A devout Hindu might find himself in an enchanted forest with Krishna. In general, what you expect in the afterlife is usually what you get, because you are magnetically attracted to the subplane that can best satisfy your needs and desires. The expression "to each his own" sums up astral conditions perfectly.

Astral Work and Play

All of our frustrated earth desires to create great and wonderful things can come to happy fruition on the astral plane. A dedicated musician is likely to find himself among other great and inspiring musicians, and the same holds true for artists, craftsmen, scientists, mathematicians, farmers, soldiers, sailors, students and so on — we all tend to congregate with souls who share the same beliefs and enthusiasms.

On the astral plane we do our work with intense concentration, for the sheer pleasure of the work and for the joy and challenge of the achievement. Then, in later earth incarnations we often channel our own astral works down to the physical plane in the forms of music, art, literature, scientific inventions, humanitarian concepts and the like.

Sports on the astral plane are unimaginably exhilarating. Although the heavy earth body weighs from about a hundred pounds on up, the astral body weighs mere ounces, with a slight center of gravity at the hips. Consequently the astral body can levitate, float, fly and perform aerial maneuvers such as flips, loops and spirals. The astral body can also easily run huge distances with long, pleasurable, floating strides. I can remember doing all of the above on the astral plane, as well as swimming (no need to hold your breath), horseback riding, flying a small airplane, skiing down a wonderful, very steep mountain, and so on. If you remember your nightly out-of-body experiences, you will probably have similar memories of the sheer delight of expressing yourself in your astral form.

Companionship on the astral plane is far more satisfying than it is on Earth for the simple reason that astral souls are linked telepathically, making communication much more rich and precise, without confusing misunderstandings. Friends and lovers share a deep bond at the soul level as each of us grows into our highest potential, both emotionally and spiritually.

Most people wonder if there is sex after death. Well, be of good cheer, for there most certainly is, and in its most lovely, exotic forms. While our dense physical bodies have only five senses, the luxurious astral body has twenty-four, and in addition to this tremendous amount of sensory input, sexual partners enjoy a special telepathic link that unites them much more intimately than is even remotely possible on Earth. On the astral plane two souls can achieve a true blending of body, mind and spirit.

Spiritually, it is possible to meet the great Ascended Masters on the astral planes. You can follow in their footsteps, sit at their feet, listen to their thoughts and experience the indescribable joy of feeling your soul expand and come to fruition under their gentle and wise guidance.

As you might guess, it would be possible to write volumes on the wealth of experiences that the soul undergoes on the astral plane, but we will have to be content here with the above suggestions. However, if you dwell on these thoughts as you meditate, it is possible that you will begin to remember some of your own astral lifetimes and build a more complete picture of the astral subplanes that you have visited.

Returning to Earth

Some souls spend just a few years on the astral plane whereas others spend one or two centuries — each according to its needs and desires. But sooner or later, just as we grow tired at the end of a long, wonderful earth day, the astral soul begins to grow languid and develops a wish for rest. When this happens the soul once again falls into a deep slumber in order to prepare for its next earth incarnation.

Just as it did after physical life, during this deep sleep the soul reviews its past astral life, taking stock of its lessons, goals and achievements. Then it begins to gather energy, lay plans for its next earth life, and receive the psychic patterns for its future earth body. Higher souls help the reincarnating soul choose the earth environment, circumstances, and parents that will best help the soul's work during the next phase of its growth.

When the time is right, the soul projects itself back down onto the physical plane to visit its new physical body in its embryonic state. Entering through the soft part of the skull (the crown chakra), the soul begins to merge the psychic patterns encoded in its spiritual DNA with the physical DNA supplied by the earth parents. The soul will exit and enter the embryonic body many times as it grows accustomed to its new vehicle, until eventually the child is born, the brain develops, bone grows over the soft portion of the skull and a permanent link is established. During childhood the soul gradually becomes fully awake and begins to manifest more and more strongly through its new body.

For those who do not return to Earth, the process is similar in that the soul also drops into a deep slumber and reviews its recent astral life. The difference is that it awakens on the mental realms, which are a step above the astral plane. It then alternates lifetimes between the astral and the mental planes, just as it formerly alternated between the physical and the astral. In this way we work our way up the ladder of spiritual planes until eventually, when we have learned all of our lessons, we graduate to another set of worlds altogether.

In closing, it should be emphasized that wherever it is, the soul is always, always, *always* precisely where it needs to be in order to fulfill its deepest desires and learn the lessons it needs for its greatest benefit.

If you would like to read more about this fascinating topic, two books that have jogged a lot of memories for me are Lead-beater's *The Astral Plane* published by the Theosophical Society, and Rama-charaka's *The Life After Death,* which may or may not still be in print — check with your local metaphysical bookstore.

USING CRYSTALS
FOR HEALING
AND MEDITATION

18

Gifts from the Angels

Suppose you were to seek out the Angels and request a very special gift from them: something that would open a wide range of metaphysical possibilities for you; something that would bring spiritual comfort and inspiration; something that would assist in the healing of body, emotions, mind and soul; something that would give you access to other worlds and other dimensions; something that would act as a wise teacher and a comfortable friend; something that would be the catalyst to change your life from the mundane to the extraordinary.

Now suppose the Angels decide to grant your request and fashion for you bits of frozen light in all the colors of the rainbow, blessing these gifts with the pure grace of their own heart chakras. If such an astonishing thing were to happen, it would surely be miraculous.

Well, this miracle has already happened and the bits of colored light are scattered generously all over the Earth. Crystals are gifts from the Angelic Kingdom to mankind. One or more Angels has consciously formed every crystal, giving each its own specific variations of color, size, shape and vibration.

In much the same way that we tend our flower gardens, the Devas (the Sanskrit word for Angels) may be seen tending earth's crystal gardens from the finer planes, except instead of watering the crystal beds, Devas channel high-frequency energy from all of the different vibrational planes down through their chakra systems and then pour that energy into the crystals. This means that the crystals and gems that balance our chakras so beautifully are actually tuned to the frequency of the Angels' own chakras. If you pause to think about it, that's rather marvelous, and it accounts for the tremendous spiritual and healing qualities that all crystals have.

By tuning your chakras and bringing focus to your inner vision, crystals can unveil glorious new worlds for you. In addition, crystals used in a vortex will act as transducers, stepping your energy up above its normal level and stepping the vortex energy down to a frequency your physical body can handle, so that both human and earth energies may blend harmoniously.

Every lightworker should have at least one crystal, and several crystals will do you a world of good. In some crystal shops you can purchase a dozen useful little crystal points for just a few dollars, or you can splurge and spend hundreds of dollars on a single unique piece. There are crystals for everyone's budget, crystals for everyone's needs. Shopping for crystals is like a treasure hunt. Not only is it a thoroughly pleasant way to spend an afternoon, but just walking into a crystal shop will cleanse your aura and raise your energy.

Crystals Work Through the Chakra System

Although many people use crystals for healing, channeling,

and meditation, most people are vague as to how crystals work. The simple fact is, crystals work through the chakra system. Physical healing is generally the result of a crystal's flooding the *lower, earth-oriented chakras* with a rush of perfectly tuned energy which enables the body's systems to clear blocks and rebalance themselves.

Using the proper crystals on the *higher chakras* fine-tunes the spiritual energies, aligns the subtle bodies and opens the psychic channels. The minute you come within range of a crystal's auric field it begins to work on your chakra system, regardless of whether you are wearing the stone, holding it, or simply standing in the same room with it.

Crystals require very little care in return for their gifts, with only three things essential to their well-being. First, your stones must be kept clean. A crystal is like a tape recorder that is always on; it is constantly picking up physical and mental vibrations thrown out by people in its vicinity. Crystals can also pick up strong thoughts and emotions from the past that have a tendency to remain in houses and buildings, as well as general negative vibrations that constantly circulate in the Earth's psychic atmosphere. Crystals not only magnify all of these images, but they rebroadcast them far and wide in an amplified form. A new crystal that you've just brought home will have picked up the vibrations of the people who mined it, the various dealers who have bought and sold it, and all of the people who have walked into the shop where it was on display. Some of these people will have been worried, angry, depressed, sick and so on. Your crystal needs to get rid of all this miscellaneous junk, or it will project it into your auric field.

Crystals may be cleaned by either soaking them overnight in salt water (sea salt is best) or by placing them on a Microcrystal Card (sold in many metaphysical shops) for about an hour — longer if the crystal is large. Microcrystal Cards are also excellent for vibrationally cleaning jewelry of all types, especially pieces that contain gems. They are not only very efficient and simpler to use than salt water, but they seem to last forever and are much easier to carry. Have you ever tried to get a quart of salt water into your purse or hip pocket while traveling? If you cannot find Microcrystal Cards in your area, call Crystal Magic at (520) 282-1622 or the Crystal Castle at (520) 282-5910.

Since crystals are, in effect, solar batteries, their second requirement is a bit of sunlight to renew their energy and keep them at their peak. *The exceptions are rose quartz, amethyst and kunzite, which will fade if exposed to direct sunlight for long periods of time.* Beware also of placing clear crystal spheres in direct sunlight, since they magnify the sun's rays and can start a fire if they are sitting on anything flammable. *When charging a crystal ball in the sun, if you place it in a shallow dish filled with a half inch or so of water, the liquid will absorb the heat from the sun's rays and will also keep the sphere from becoming too hot internally.*

Lastly, care needs to be taken not to chip or break your stones. Just as your soul inhabits your physical body, so crystals have an indwelling spirit and they feel pain acutely. In addition, crystals have chakras, so a break is liable to result in the loss of one or more energy centers, leaving the crystal clouded with pain and less able to serve you. If you take good care of your crystals, they will take good care of you. They will also offer you companionship if you are open to it. Most people who work intensively with crystals will tell you that indwelling spirits are definitely "in there," and those who take the time to get to know their crystals will find that they make superb teachers as well as charming, faithful friends. In addition, crystals have innocent, cheerful personalities that are delightfully refreshing in this imbalanced world.

19

Choosing the Right Crystals

Just as a pregnant woman might crave spinach or oranges to correct a vitamin deficiency that could hinder her developing child, so your body and superconscious mind know which crystal vibrations will be beneficial to your growing spirit. This generally manifests as a strong attraction to a particular type of crystal or to a specific individual stone. But with the multitude of crystals available, sometimes the choice is overwhelming. So let's take a look at some of the differences among them.

Natural Crystals versus
Tumbled Stones and Faceted Gems

With the exception of man-made lead crystal, which closes the chakras because of its lead content, all types of crystals are valuable for metaphysical and spiritual development, whether they are single natural points, clusters, tumbled stones, polished meta-tools or cut gems. The basic differences have to do with energy output.

Naturally terminated crystals, including clusters, focus a stream of energy out through their points much like water flowing from a hose. Therefore, a naturally terminated crystal is used primarily to move energy. If you have such a crystal or see one in a shop that attracts you, try rubbing your hands briskly together until you generate a lot of heat, and then wave the pointed end of the crystal an inch above the palm and fingers of your left hand. Do you feel a tingle? That tingle is the energy generated by the stone, and you will notice that different crystals produce different sensations. This energy is what crystals are all about.

The energy of tumbled stones and polished meta-tools tends to be more stationary. To clairvoyant vision such energy looks like a bright aura of light surrounding the stone. Colored tumbled stones are used to provide specific frequencies of vibration, such as red-spectrum energy or green and the like. Tumbled stones also provide an inexpensive source of wonderful crystals that would be much more costly in their cut forms.

As opposed to the irregular shapes of tumbled stones, the specific shapes of the various meta-tools have a great deal to do with their functions. A pyramid cut generates energy; a sphere focuses clairvoyant energy and helps deepen concentration; an egg shape is comforting and healing to hold; and wands direct energy if they are formed from naturally terminated crystals. If they are made out of a plain chunk of crystal, a strongly directed thought will usually send the wand's energy wherever you wish it to go.

A faceted gem flings out brilliant geometrical patterns of energy as light enters the stone, bounces around from facet to facet gathering intensity, and eventually radiates back out of the gem in strong symmetrical lines and planes. Because of this intensification, the energy field around a nicely faceted stone is tremendous, even if the stone is quite small. Clarity, color and faceting determine the vibrational frequency of gems; transparent, brightly colored stones with symmetrical, intricate facets are the most power-ful. Blue and violet gems of this nature are highly desirable for meditation. Use them on the third eye chakra to tune, balance, energize and evolve this psychic center all at the same time. Larger gems are exceptionally effective for healing work because the symmetry of their energy patterns — coupled with their high intensity — tends to snap imbalanced chakras back into a state of rhythm and harmony.

For healing or meditation, all of the above types of stones are useful. A combination of natural and tumbled stones, plus a gem or two, is one of the most effective ways to balance chakras. A few inexpensive tumbled stones arranged in geometric patterns over the chakras will tune each chakra to its perfect color fre-quency (use red stones on the first chakra, orange on the second, and so on); natural quartz points between the chakras will move the kundalini energy up from chakra to chakra; and a small gem over the third eye will give you the maximum tuning for clairvoy-ance.

Even if your budget forces you to choose small stones, do not underestimate their energy potential. If we could tap into it to-tally, there would be enough energy in one grain of common quartz sand to run all of New York City for a year — toasters, taxi-cabs, computers — the works. With that in mind, what do you suppose a two-inch crystal could do, or a two-pounder? Further-more, the energy field around a half-inch crystal is something on the order of three feet in every direction, and the distance increases by geometric increments as the crystals get larger. The huge earth-keeper crystals literally energize hundreds of square miles. An average pendant-sized crystal could probably run North Amer-ica for a year or two, so don't think that a small stone can't accomplish whatever you need it to do.

Crystal Jewelry

Crystal jewelry is not only attractive and "in," but it is very practical as well. If the proper crystal is worn in the proper place, it will balance and energize your auric field as it steadily raises your vibrations. All you have to do is be certain that the crystal you choose to wear is compatible with the chakra it is worn near. Clear quartz is excellent for any part of the body, but if you are wearing a colored stone, give some thought to the color you choose. Earrings, for example, should harmonize with the blues, violets and golds that characterize the energy field around the head. A short necklace would do well to have a crystal that is beneficial to the throat, or at least one that will not close the throat chakra down. For example, an orange or red stone at the throat will tend to shut the chakra, and with constant use could result in problems. As a general rule of thumb, the first chakra is closed by green, the second by blue, the navel and the solar plexus by violet and blue, the throat is closed by orange, the third eye by red. The heart and crown chakras are not closed by any color. If a chakra is overactive, sometimes it is helpful to close it a bit; blue on the solar plexus, for example, can soothe emotional agitation.

Since the hands connect to the heart energy, stones of any color are good for rings. Remember that the left hand receives energy, while the right hand sends energy out, so if you wish to bathe yourself in the vibrations of a particular stone, it should be worn on the left hand. If, however, you wish to project the energy of your ring stone to someone else, as a healer might, it would be more advantageous to wear the stone on the right hand.

The most efficient place to wear a crystal or gem is right at the heart chakra, where all colors are beneficial. Since the heart center balances the entire auric field, a crystal worn in this area supplies energy to the whole physical system as well as to all of the subtle bodies. As an example, a person wishing to wear a stone that will work on his or her second-chakra energy would find it inconvenient and uncomfortable to tape a stone in that region. But if the appropriate stone were worn over the heart, its energy would circulate to the second chakra and work just as effectively.

One word of caution: it is frequently advisable to wear your heart stones under your clothing, since bending over a counter or desk can badly chip a crystal if it swings down and strikes a hard surface.

All crystals and gems worn as jewelry need to be cleaned often, as do healing stones. Once a week is a must for jewelry, and don't forget to promptly clean any crystals you might be wearing after a trying day or any kind of emotional crisis. Otherwise the stones will radiate the negativity back to you, with a tendency to reproduce the same unsettling emotions over and over again. This is how many famous gems have come by their reputations as unlucky stones. It is also wise to clean your jewelry after visiting a hospital, a bar or any other establishment with unsettling vibrations.

There are some crystals that should not be worn by certain people. Persons with hypertension or frayed nerves should be cautious about using red or orange stones. Also, both amethyst and smoky quartz put out an ultrasonic vibration, as does the combination of azurite and malachite in the same stone. This ultrasonic vibration is helpful in small doses, but too much use can harm your etheric body. Lastly, many nervous people find that highly electrical stones are disquieting if they are worn too often, so be careful with topaz and the tourmaline family.

Laser crystals should never, ever be worn. These crystals are like surgical blades that will slice through your aura in a matter of seconds. If they are worn they can do severe damage to your chakras and auric field, so avoid them in jewelry at all costs, and if you see someone else wearing one, tell her/him. Lasers should also be kept away from pets and children. If you handle them exactly as if they were scalpels or razor blades, you'll have the right idea. If you don't know what a laser looks like, now is the time to learn. Generally, they are naturally terminated clear quartz crystals with shabby looking, curved or bent sides and extremely tiny terminal faces which come to a very small point (as opposed to the larger, flat terminal faces of a regular crystal point). If you think of the shape of an icicle dripping down to a fine point, you will have the image of a laser crystal. Other types of crystal such as smoky quartz can also take this form. Should you buy such a crystal, treat it with respect and don't point it at yourself or anyone else.

Finally, probably no one will want to hear this, but here it is, anyway: please be very careful not to overdo it with your crystals. You should not wear crystals every day, and you should not sleep very often with stones in the bedroom . . . their energy is simply too penetrating. Although the first few times you sleep with crystals you will feel great and probably sleep magnificently, constant overexposure to crystals weakens the chakras, blitzes the psychic centers, tears the etheric body and undermines the health. A little crystal energy goes a long, long way. You will find that a few short sessions with crystals are much more powerful than constantly immersing yourself in crystal energy. If you are using crystal jewelry, from one to three days a week is more than sufficient to keep yourself well-tuned. Anything more than that can do more harm than good. So please don't trash yourself with way too much of a good thing. Remember, the Great White Brotherhood needs you . . . intact.

20

Making a Master Healing Crystal

With rapidly rising energies flooding the planet, many people are experiencing new spiritual awakenings, and those who are already awake are moving higher and deeper into the spectacular inner realms. At this time many powerful new healing and meditation tools are being channeled down into our dimensions from the Angelic planes in order to assist with the spiritual work being done here. Among these tools are the Master Healing Crystals.

The concept behind Master Healing Crystals is simple: A painting or photo of the face of a Spiritual Master is affixed to the back of a clear, well-formed crystal (usually quartz), with the face of the Master looking into the crystal. When the crystal is viewed from the front, it appears as if the Master is inside the crystal. If the crystal has an interesting combination of facets, the Master's portrait will be mirrored several times inside the crystal, giving an unusual multidimensional effect. Since the Masters' personal energies are channeled through their portraits, the combination of Master-plus-crystal results in a tool that throws out bolts of radiant spiritual, mental, emotional and physical energy. Not only do these energies bear the stamp of the particular Master's vibration, conducted and amplified by the crystal, but at the same time the crystal's own special attributes are also wonderfully augmented by the Master's energy. A beautiful Master Crystal with a portrait of the Divine Mother may be seen on the back cover of this book.

Whole sets of these crystals can be made easily and relatively inexpensively, depending on the quality of the stones. Imagine, for example, the potential of a set of several Master Crystals placed in geometric patterns around the body or on the chakras. Imagine yourself surrounded and infused with the living Light of several Masters: what would it be like to have the combined energies of three Spiritual Masters flowing through your physical and subtle bodies all at once? Or to have a crystal bearing your own guru's amplified vibration on each of your chakras? Such experiences can take you higher than you've ever been in meditation, or to a deeper healing level than you've ever achieved.

Making a Master Crystal is an adventure that anyone can enjoy. Begin by tracking down the perfect picture (preferably in color) of your chosen Master. If the picture is too large to fit on an average crystal, the size can be altered by making a colored photocopy reduction.

When you shop for your crystal, take the Master's portrait with you and plan a leisurely search. Depending on the size of your Master portrait, you might wind up using a very large quartz crystal for mega-power, or a small, very fine crystal such as a Herkimer, clear topaz, light amethyst, pale rose quartz, citrine, or any other pale-colored, very clear, gem-quality crystal that will provide an elegant, specialized energy.

You may have to look through dozens and dozens of crystals before you find just the right one. Rest assured the Master is over your shoulder, guiding you to the best find. As you look, place each candidate stone right on top of the Master's portrait and notice carefully how the Master's face shines through the crystal. Rotate the crystal to see which facet is best against the photo. If the crystal is just right, no major flaws will obscure the portrait and the Master's features will show clearly through the crystal. The effect should be undistorted and delicate. If the crystal is super-right, almost every facet will reflect the Master's face at the same time. It is possible to have three to six faces of a Master appear simultaneously in a crystal. Master/crystal combinations such as these are awesome to see, and the energies are pure magic. So even if it takes a long time to find the right stone, the result will be well worth your time, effort and money.

After you get your chosen crystal home, either soak it in sea salt water for three days or place it on a Microcrystal Card or one of the similar pink plates for twenty-four hours to clean the crystal vibrationally. Then energize the cleansed crystal in the sun for several hours until you feel it is charged and sparkling.

Next, you will need a strong, clear-drying white glue such as Elmer's to affix the portrait to the crystal. *Although it's tempting, do not use epoxy or any other non-water-soluble glue for this, as they are toxic to the chakras.* Determine precisely where you wish to place the Master's portrait on the back of the crystal, then carefully trim it to the appropriate size and shape. Next, take a small, soft brush (such as a watercolor brush or a small makeup brush) and carefully apply a thin, even layer of glue *right on the Master's face.* Cover the whole piece of paper from edge to edge, then quickly press the portrait face down on the chosen (back) facet of the crystal. Run your fingers over the portrait repeatedly to smooth out any bubbles, unglued areas, etc. If you find any such raised places, smooth them out as best you can with your fingers — if you don't, you will get shiny blank spots that will obscure parts of the portrait. (If you are uncertain about this part of the process, practice first with any picture cut out of a magazine so you can see how the glue behaves and how to avoid bubbles. After you have finished with the practice photo, soak it off in water, dry the crystal, and then affix the Master's portrait.)

When you are satisfied with your results, simply let the glue dry. If there is print on the reverse of your portrait or if the back of the photo is unappealing, you can glue colored foil or paper, or perhaps apply a little acrylic paint to the back of the portrait to give it a more finished look.

Your Master Healing Crystal is now ready to go, and with care should give you years of healing and meditation energy. Master Crystals may be used for just about any metaphysical endeavor: they are excellent for meditation, channeling, deep concentration, prayer, astral projection, telepathy, healing, balancing, energizing and long-distance work. If you are uncertain as to how to use your crystal in various situations, listen to your inner guidance.

Caring for Your Master Crystal

From here on out, if you place your crystal in the sun to energize it, be sure to put it on its side so the sun does not shine directly through the crystal onto the Master's portrait, which could fade it over a period of time. Cleaning the crystal in saltwater is, of course, no longer possible at this point. Try covering the crystal in dry sea salt or putting it on a Microcrystal Card or pink plate (sold for $7 to $10 in many metaphysical shops) for about fifteen minutes. A soft silk or velvet pouch is recommended to keep your crystal safe and clean when traveling. When you are at home, an altar is an ideal place for your Master Crystal when it is not in use.

21

Build Your Own Vortex: Temple Jewel Power Tools and Light Boxes

This chapter will consider crystals and gems as units of pure energy that can be combined into simple and complex patterns, forming dazzling vortices of power. All you need is a few dollars, a little ingenuity and some spare time.

Temple Jewel Power Tools

A Temple Jewel Power Tool is a glass disk which is covered with small quartz crystals and gems placed in a geometric design. Disks such as this create powerful vortexes of astral light which are superb for chakra balancing. After working with one or more of these disks you will find that the elegant geometry formed by the stones builds dynamic patterns of energy that spiral down into the chakras like bolts of colored lightning, opening, balancing cleansing, tuning and healing as they go.

Of course, you can also place the stones directly on the chakras, as discussed elsewhere; this method allows you to change stones, crystals and patterns freely. But the disadvantage is that stones placed on the body are liable to lose their position and/or roll off, which weakens the efficiency of the pattern. Stones that are actually glued onto a piece of glass, on the other hand, will retain their relative positions and they offer many more possibilities for intricate patterning.

If you were to try to buy such chakra tools ready-made the price would be prohibitive, but by shopping around you should be able to assemble several nice Temple Jewel Power Tools for a moderate amount of money. Begin with a trip to your local stained-glass shop and purchase a few disks of clear, round, beveled glass; these are inexpensive circles of glass that are flat on one side and on the other side are slightly raised in the center and beveled toward the edges. The bevel is not necessary for our purposes, but this type of glass is cheap and readily available, so it will do unless you have access to something you like better. At any rate, the bevels come in several shapes and diameters; the two- and three- inch-round sizes are best for chakra work. This glass is what you will mount your crystals on.

Next, treat yourself to a trip to your local rock shop or, better yet, a gem and mineral show. Try to find some very small natural quartz points and an assortment of tumbled stones. Sometimes you can even find a real bargain such as a bag of twenty small, faceted gems for $50 or so. In an earlier column we discussed the various cuts of stones and the energy they put out. Let's recapitulate by saying that quartz points move energy; faceted stones radiate colored energy in precise geometric patterns; and tumbled stones make a little halo of highly specialized colored energy.

If you are near an antique store or a sewing shop, you can sometimes find inexpensive costume jewelry or bags of colored faceted glass that you can use instead of gems. If these fake gems are perfectly transparent, they can be pried out of their setting and used on your disk. Since most glass is made of quartz, the vibration will be very smooth. Caution: *Do not use leaded glass or leaded Austrian crystal, as lead shuts down the chakras.*

Once you have your basic materials, you need only a little white glue such as Elmer's (avoid epoxy or anything else that would be toxic to your chakras; white, water-soluble glue is the only safe thing to use) and a pair of tweezers.

To assemble your disk, start by cleaning the beveled glass. Now you need a geometric pattern of some sort to serve as a template for the crystals. You can either draw your own or use the templates at the end of this chapter.

These patterns will allow you to place the crystals very precisely on or between the lines and on their intersections. It helps if you make a rough crystal arrangement ahead of time, experimenting with different designs until you find one you like. (Tip: For pattern ideas, look at pictures of stained-glass windows or look into a kaleidoscope.) Then place your beveled glass over the template and begin to glue your crystals down. Tweezers will help you place the stones precisely. Use your small clear quartz points or Herkimer diamonds to move energy, and your tumbled or faceted gems to key into whichever chakra you wish to work on. To choose stones for a specific chakra, consult with Gurudas' wonderful book, *Gem Elixirs and Vibrational Healing, Vol. 1,* or some other reliable crystal reference.

To make an all-purpose energizing pattern that can be tuned to every chakra, use only clear quartz and/or Herkimers, with no stone in the center. If you use the disk on the first chakra, place a garnet in the center (a tiny dab of honey will glue it in place temporarily); replace the garnet with amethyst or lapis for the third eye; watermelon tourmaline or rose quartz for the heart, and so on.

When your pattern is finished, wait overnight for the glue to dry and then clean the disk vibrationally on a Microcrystal Card or high up in the smoke of sandalwood, cedar or sage incense (being careful not to scorch the disk or yourself). Then lie back and put the disk on the intended chakra. Wait a few minutes for the disk to connect with your chakra, then feel the action as the crystal pattern begins its balancing, tuning and energizing work.

Between sessions, store your disks in a box to keep them free of dust and lint. When necessary, clean them carefully with a damp cotton swab. You may use your disks on other people if you wish, providing you clean them well vibrationally with incense and/or a Microcrystal Card after each use. Otherwise, the crystals will pick up trauma and emotional debris from one person and radiate them in amplified form back into someone else the next time you use the disk. If you are using the disk only on yourself, you should still clean it vibrationally after each use so you don't pour your own old junk back into your system. Be sure to clean oil from your skin off the bottom of the disk after each use. *In order for the finer energies to flow well, the disks must be very clean.*

Light Boxes

Light boxes are an old Atlantean and Lemurian device used to broadcast crystal energy throughout a house, temple or any other large space. You can usually buy a large to medium sized light box at a printers' or art supply store, or at a photography shop. Then go to your local rock shop and have a field day buying lots of tumbled stones, small quartz crystals and whatever other types of stone seem attractive. Or you can go to your stained glass shop and get a bunch of the beautiful small glass nuggets that come in all the brilliant colors of the rainbow.

Next, combine your tumbled stones or glass nuggets with a few quartz crystals, building an intricate geometric pattern on top of the light box. Turn on the lamp and you will have a dynamic energy field that will fill your house with a huge column of exquisite astral light patterns. If you are very clairvoyant, you will perhaps be able to see the column of light; if not, you should begin to feel it after a few minutes. This wonderful energy is excellent for meditation, channeling, healing or deep concentration. When you are tired of one pattern, change it. Your designs can be as simple or as intricate as you like, but your choice of stones is important. For example, you can fill your home with heart energy, channeling or meditation energy, healing energy, and so on simply by picking the appropriate crystals. The Gurudas book mentioned above is an unerring guide to the vibrational properties of crystals.

Warning

All of these vortex patterns are extremely powerful. A disk should be left on a chakra for no more than twenty minutes a day, and a light box should not be left on for more than sixty minutes a day. If you exceed these time limits the energy will be too much for the physical body and it will start to overload your chakras. A chakra overload can set you way, way back in your development, so be careful. Many people tend to think that twenty to sixty minutes might be enough for other people but not for them. This attitude is extremely foolish and will definitely do more harm than good. The above time limits are calculated to give you the maximum benefits; longer times will shut you down. Also, if you have hypertension, avoid using red and orange stones, as they can raise the blood pressure.

Temple Jewel Templates

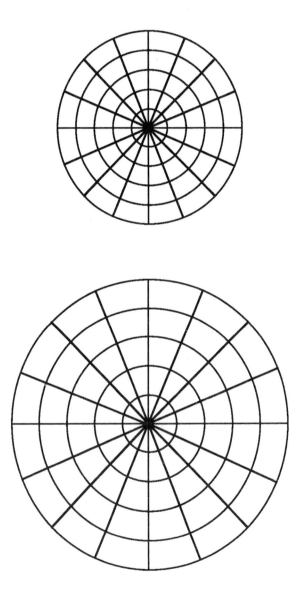

22

Three Excellent Crystal Balances

Every serious student of metaphysics needs to know how to do a chakra balance. It is as necessary as keeping your car in tune: if you wish to travel and sightsee on the higher planes, you must have your vehicle in good repair and running smoothly.

Following are three balances that anyone can do. In fact, the trick is not so much to do the balances, but to keep from *overdoing* them. Metaphysical work is so much easier with crystals on your chakras that there is a temptation to use too many stones too often. But since the effects of a full chakra balance last for three to six weeks, balancing more often than that will spoil the maturing effects of the previous balance and risk burning out your delicate psychic energies. Moderation is the key here, as it always is with deep-level metaphysical work. Remember to give the body an adequate chance to catch up with the spirit.

A Simple Mini-Balance

This is an easy balance and it has the advantage of being inexpensive and quick. You will need just one clear quartz generator crystal (a naturally occurring crystal point) that is at least two inches long. Be sure the crystal is clean and charged by the sun; you don't want to put miscellaneous junk into your chakras with a crystal that hasn't been cleared, and if the crystal isn't energized, it can't energize you.

To begin, sit in a comfortable position and breathe in deeply five or six times to relax your physical body and to strengthen its connection with the soul. Next, hold the point of the crystal to your base chakra, and as you inhale visualize that you are breathing waves of crystal energy in through the chakra, pulling it all the way back to the tip of the spine. Picture the crystal energy as cascades of sparkling white light flowing out of the crystal the way water gushes out of a garden hose. Breathe this energy in three or four times with concentration; then move up to the second chakra and repeat the process. When you have finished with the second chakra, work your way carefully up to the navel, solar plexus, heart, throat, third eye and crown chakras, pulling the crystal energy from the stone straight back into the spine each time. When you get to the third eye and crown, pull the crystal energy inside your skull, visualizing it filling your mind with soft white light.

After you have energized each chakra, bring your generator crystal back down to the first chakra and then slowly sweep it straight up past every chakra all the way to the crown. Do this six to ten times. If you are sensitive to crystal energy and if your crystal is well charged, you will feel a flushing sensation of warmth filling your body as the kundalini energy rises to follow the crystal's path. If you do not notice this heat, don't worry about it — the energy is there whether you can feel it or not.

An Intermediate Balance

This balance is fairly simple and inexpensive, but it takes longer than the mini-balance because it is more thorough. For this balance you will need a quartz generator as in the mini-balance, plus seven or eight smaller one-inch quartz points. You will also need a grounding stone: a small black tourmaline or smoky quartz will do nicely. Without the grounding stone you will drift off into la-la land and be unable to focus your psychic energies.

Start by lying down on your back, and when you are comfortably positioned put the grounding crystal on your first chakra, pointing toward your feet. Next, put one clear quartz crystal on each chakra, with all of their points toward your head. (Add one to the base chakra also, above the grounding stone.) Arrange all of the stones in a nice straight line so the energy will relay easily from crystal to crystal. Lastly, put the eighth crystal on the floor above your head with its tip pointing up away from your body.

Now follow the same procedure that was given for the mini-balance. Breathe in deeply five or six times to start pulling energy down from the soul and subtle bodies. Then hold your generator crystal to each chakra, starting at the base, and breathe in light from the stones several times, pulling the energy from the front of the body straight back to the spine. Finish by using the generator in a sweeping motion up past all of the chakras six to ten times. This will start the energy flow up the spine and begin linking the chakras. It will also align the subtle bodies with the physical body.

When the last step is completed, close your eyes and relax. You can either continue to hold your generator crystal in your hand or, if you do not have a crystal above the crown chakra, you can put the generator there, pointing up and aligned with the body.

The stones should be left on your chakras for fifteen to forty-five minutes. This is an excellent time to meditate and/or channel, because you have just raised your psychic antennae in an extremely powerful manner and your metaphysical abilities will be at their peak.

A Full Balance

If you feel your energy is seriously out of tune; if you are tired or recuperating from an illness; if you have been through a period of stress; or if you wish to do some extra-deep metaphysical or spiritual exploring, this balance is superb. It is similar to the intermediate balance in that it uses the same stones and the same procedure. The difference is that in addition to the quartz generator, the seven or eight small quartz points, and the grounding stone, you will also put tumbled stones, gems or colored glass on the chakras to fine-tune their energy to the correct frequencies.

Crystal shops are full of inexpensive tumbled stones and small, rough crystals of many types. These stones are wonderful for chakra balancing and will give you all the power you need and much more. Twenty to fifty dollars will buy you a large selection of tumbled or raw stones such as garnet or ruby for the first chakra; carnelian or citrine for the second chakra; pyrite or peridot for the navel; aquamarine or lepidolite for the solar plexus; emerald or pink and green tourmaline for the heart chakra; turquoise or blue topaz for the throat; sapphire or lapis for the third eye; and amethyst or sugilite for the crown chakra. Other wonderful stones include calcite, malachite, rhodochrosite, rhodonite, dioptase, rose quartz, Herkimer diamonds, azurite, fluorite, celestite, amazonite, apatite, chrysocolla, tiger's eye, selenite, and sodalite. If you have a diamond ring, clean it well vibrationally and try it above the crown chakra or on the solar plexus. Gurudas' book, Gem Elixirs and Vibrational Healing, Vol. 1, will tell you all about the qualities of each stone. His information is totally reliable.

An alternative to colored stones may be found in almost any stained-glass shop. Ask for the glass nuggets that come in various bright, jewel-like colors, ranging in size from a nickel to a silver dollar. These nuggets are flat on the bottom and rounded on top like cabochon gemstones. The colors are awesome: clear, deep ruby red, sapphire blue, topaz yellow, emerald green, peridot green, amethyst purple, citrine orange and a beautiful black that makes a nice grounding stone. Because their colors are so gorgeous and pure, these glass nuggets are marvelous for tuning chakras to the perfect vibration. They are also refreshingly inexpensive.

You may want to assign one colored stone or piece of glass to each chakra, matching the color of the stone to the color of the chakra. A general rule of thumb for your primary stone on each chakra is red for the first chakra, orange for the second, yellow for the navel, clear or lime green for the solar plexus, any color for the heart (but especially green), pale blue for the throat, deep blue or indigo for the third eye and violet for the crown. Or you may decide to add several stones of different colors to each chakra, depending on your resources. The decision is up to you — go with your intuition and guidance. Just be sure the colors of the stones on any given chakra look good together. This assures you that their energies are compatible with one another. If the colors of two stones clash, so do their energies, and you would not want to put a discordant combination on a chakra.

Most chakras will require only one colored stone/glass for tuning, but if you feel a particular chakra needs a lot of work, then use more stones on it, preferably in a geometric arrangement. This is a very individual thing and no two people would be likely to pick the same combination of crystals. It's a safe bet that what appeals to you is right for you, so trust your intuition and give full rein to your creativity. It's a little like cooking — a sprinkle of this and a dash of that, and presto! something wonderful and indescribable happens.

If you opt for a geometric arrangement, a very powerful combination is four stones (above, below, to the left and to the right of the chakra) with a fifth stone in the center. For example, how about a rough emerald in the center of the heart chakra and four rough rubies around it? Or a piece of green glass in the center with four red nuggets around that? If you are flat-chested (a great virtue in crystal work!) you can do quite elaborate patterns with twelve or more crystals or pieces of glass. The balancing that takes place under such circumstances is exquisite.

To begin your balance, lie down and arrange the colored stones on each chakra, with the clear quartz crystals between the chakras (pointing toward the head) and the grounding stone low on the first chakra or below the feet. The colored pieces will tune each chakra and the clear quartz will move energy up the spine from chakra to chakra.

When all the stones are in place, proceed as in the first two balances, inhaling deeply several times and then breathing the energy from the stones in through each chakra straight back to the spine. Next, link the chakras by slowly moving your quartz generator above the stones from the first chakra to the crown several times. As you might guess, this is easier with two people, so find an accomplice if you can.

When you have finished, close your eyes and relax for thirty minutes or so, taking advantage of your greatly heightened metaphysical awareness to meditate, channel, problem-solve or watch for old memories to surface.

When you feel the time is right, remove the stones. If you're a little groggy or spacy, move away from the crystals and hold the grounding stone in your left hand for a few minutes until you come back down to Earth. Then be sure to clean your crystals vibrationally with incense or a Microcrystal Card so they can release any stress they might have picked up from your chakras. If you use incense, hold your stones high up in the smoke, so as not to scorch yourself or your crystals.

You will find that a balance does not end when the crystals come off. On the contrary, the energy will flow strongly within your physical and subtle bodies for weeks to come. During this time delicate connections will begin to be made in the central nervous system, so two weeks down the road you may suddenly find yourself much more together than you ever were before. After a strong crystal balance some people begin to work at exciting new depths, seeing, channeling or visiting entirely different realms of awareness, while others expand their creative healing, writing or artwork into deeply fulfilling dimensions they have never before experienced.

23

Crystals as
Fragments of the
Divine Mind

Metaphysical thought holds that everything that exists is made of mind matter formed from the thought energy of the Divine Power. The chair you are sitting on is mind matter; this book is mind matter; you are mind matter; so are the Earth, the Universe and all of infinity. Some of this mind matter is dormant; some is fully awakened; most is somewhere in between. Encumbered as we are by our dense physical bodies, human beings tend to be half-dormant, going through daily tasks like sleepwalkers, with very little conscious awareness of the spiritual dimensions. The pursuit of metaphysics is an attempt to awaken our dormant mind matter, raise our level of conscious awareness, and begin to merge our somewhat murky individual consciousness with the awesome splendor and unlimited clarity of pure Divine Consciousness.

Crystals are a vital link in our search for this spiritual enlightenment, because they act as transducers — that is to say, they are capable of raising our mental energies up into the divine spheres, as well as stepping sublime higher energies down to our physical level. Some people resist hearing it, but crystals are also highly conscious entities, with all of the traits of sentient beings. Crystals think, experience emotion, feel pain and have hopes and dreams just as we do. If that sounds far-fetched to you, consider this: our brains run on silica. Quartz crystals are composed of silicon dioxide . . . they are really a very pure form of mind matter. What all of this boils down to is the fact that crystals are every bit as intelligent as we are, and perhaps much more so. If you're having trouble believing this, read on!

At this point I would like to share with you some of my telepathic experiences with crystals — personal lessons that have come to me as part of my own spiritual growth. I invite you to share some of these experiences with me, then become more sensitive to your own crystals, and then judge for yourself whether indwelling spirits are there or not.

Lotus

Living with me is a beautiful amethyst sphere named Lotus. Most of her is deep, clear purple; the rest is a mystical light lavender. Her energy is truly sublime. One day about six months after I bought Lotus, I found a larger amethyst sphere in a crystal shop; it was deep purple through and through, which was what I had originally been looking for before I found Lotus. That evening I was standing at the sink doing dishes, wondering if I should trade Lotus in for the deeper purple sphere, wondering whether the shop owner would accept a trade plus cash, and so on. As I was thinking these things, all of a sudden a bolt of thought came crashing into my heart chakra. The thought was filled with such sadness and despair that it froze me in mid-motion. This sensation grew and grew, so I quickly sat down to meditate. I could tell a friend was in trouble emotionally, but I didn't know who. I cleared my thoughts and waited. Again my mind and heart were washed in sorrow. Someone was in agony, wondering, *"What did I do wrong? Why does she want to trade me? Is she not happy with me? She's never traded anyone else. I thought she was pleased with me. . . ."* Beyond any shadow of a doubt, it was Lotus!

Well, what can I say? I've been apologizing to her ever since. I have no idea where the larger sphere wound up, but Lotus lives in my bedroom, safe and secure in the knowledge that she will *never* be traded.

Several years after this incident, the Divine Mother had been showing me in meditation how the Angels create and modify crystal molecular structures, colors and so on. So one day after meditation, Lotus caught my eye and it occurred to me to ask her telepathically if she remembered the Angels who had been present when she was formed. I made my mind blank and waited for an answer . . . and waited . . . and waited. No answer. "Oh well," I thought, and went on with the day.

But later that night as I was sleeping, there came into my superconscious mind an exquisite fourth-dimensional holographic vision. I saw seven or eight female Angels in flowing gowns, holding hands in a circle high above a crystal bed. Their auric fields were purple with lavender tints. Slowly the ring of Angels began to spin, gathering more and more speed, forming a shaft of brilliant purple-lavender light in the center of their circle. And then suddenly the shaft of light shot down through the crystal bed, permeating it with specific color frequencies and molecular patterns. When I woke up from this intense vision, there was Lotus on her shelf by my bed — looking rather pleased, I thought.

Little Hero

Hero is a very small, clear, double-terminated Herkimer diamond, but he didn't get his name until after the incident I am about to relate. Now, this little Herkimer is wonderful on the third eye and small enough to be combined with other stones into a powerful geometric pattern on the forehead. About a year after I got him I was doing many elaborate crystal balances, helping people to remember and clear past life trauma. In these balances I would generally use from thirty to forty crystals on the client's chakras, and after each balance I would clean the crystals by covering them with sea salt. This was before I discovered Microcrystal Cards.

One day I had finished with one client and had only about fifteen minutes until the next client was due to arrive. Quickly I covered the crystals from the first balance — including the small Herkimer — with sea salt, gulped down a sandwich for dinner, and started selecting crystals for the second balance. Since I needed to reuse some of the crystals from the first balance, I quickly felt around in the bowl of sea salt and pulled out all of the crystals. As I was dumping the sea salt into the kitchen wastebasket, in walked the second client. We proceeded with his balance, after which I was tired, so I spent the rest of the evening relaxing.

About four days later I was walking through the kitchen when a very high-frequency wail stopped me in my tracks. Someone was definitely in distress and very frightened. There flashed into my mind a beautiful tiny little nonhuman face of pure dazzling light, drenched in tears of light. I panicked. So as always, I sat down to tune in and almost instantly realized I was seeing the little Herkimer diamond. I went to the box I keep him in. He was gone. I searched everywhere — no Herkimer. When had I last seen him? And where?

All of a sudden I realized I hadn't seen him for several days, and I couldn't remember taking him out of the salt with the other crystals. What if he had been thrown out with the salt? I looked in the garbage can. Yuck! I shot a thought to the Divine Mother. "Should I do it?" She smiled and said, "Yes, you'd better do it, and quickly, too!" I looked again at the stuff in the garbage can. Double yuck! "Are you sure?" I asked. I saw a picture in my head of the Divine Mother raising an eyebrow and smiling. So I plunked myself down in the middle of the kitchen floor and began excavating layer after layer of garbage. More sobbing was coming into my mind from the tiny Herkimer, so I looked and looked and looked. At the very bottom of the mess was a bunch of sea salt and coffee grounds, nothing else. Frantically I ran my fingers through the damp grunge, searching and searching. Suddenly, there was the Herkimer, safe and sound again! As I sat there clutching that precious little stone, the Divine Mother said, "At first he thought maybe you had put him in this new place on purpose and that you would come for him later. But as time passed he got more and more worried. Every time you walked by, his heart lifted as he waited for you to pick him up, but you just kept going. Then he started sending you polite, soft little thoughts, just to remind you of him, but you were preoccupied and didn't hear him. Finally, he was so stressed that he couldn't hold it in anymore, and that's when you heard him sobbing."

"Mother," I said, "what can I do to help him get over this?"

She answered, "Spend some time with him. Hold him to your heart chakra, cuddle him, talk to him and tell him his name is now Little Hero. Explain to him that he has learned a very important lesson: that no matter where he is, no matter how bleak or terrible the circumstances, someone will *always* be there to hear him and to rescue him." "And," she added, "needless to say, that same thought holds true for everyone else as well."

Today Little Hero is retired from balancing work. He lives a life of leisure and security in his little plastic box (referred to as his condo), surrounded by his consorts — a lovely selection of equally tiny crystals of several different types given especially to him by Wayne Riney at the Kokopelli crystal shop, who was touched by his story and didn't want him ever to be alone again. Don't you just love a happy ending?

The Lesson in Pain

This last anecdote involves a handful of small clear quartz crystals. One winter evening I was sitting at the table making a Temple Jewel Power Tool. This involved gluing precise, complex geometric patterns of crystals and gems onto a glass disk in order to form a powerful energy vortex; the disk could then be easily and quickly put on a chakra and used for advanced psychic work. The particular pattern I was working with involved about twenty colored stones and eight small, well-matched quartz crystals. I had placed the first two quartz crystals on the disk, but the third quartz crystal was just a bit too long. So I picked up a pair of needle-nosed pliers and snapped a tiny jagged piece of quartz off the base of the crystal. Immediately, I heard the Divine Mother say, "Please don't do that!" I absent-mindedly nodded and continued with my work. By the time I had gotten to the eighth quartz crystal, I was again concentrating deeply on the pattern and had totally forgotten the incident. Without thinking, I reached for the pliers and snipped off another irregular bit of crystal. Again I heard the Divine Mother: "Please, please, please don't do that!" Suddenly I focused on what she was saying and realized I was actually *hurting* the crystal. So I stopped to meditate for a while, and since I firmly believe that experience is the very best teacher, I decided to ask the Divine Mother if she could duplicate the quartz crystals' pain in my own body so I could have better empathy with crystals. She asked me if I was certain I wanted to do this, and I confirmed that I was.

The next morning when I woke up, a finger that I had nicked while I was making the disk was swollen and painful. The day after that the finger was badly infected and nothing would clear it up. About ten days later it had finally started to show signs of healing when I inadvertently bashed it into something and the whole agonizing infection started up all over again. All in all, it hurt for about three weeks, with pain shooting all the way up into the wrist, elbow and shoulder, and since the tip of the finger with all of its nerve endings was involved, it was truly excruciating.

The lesson was clear: The first ten days totaled the pain the first crystal had suffered, and the rest of the time represented the pain of the second crystal. Needless to say, I have handled all of my crystals very, very carefully ever since. Before long I started making a completely different type of Power Tool.

The Moral of the Story

Be kind to your crystals and avoid damaging them even slightly — being dropped is especially traumatic for them. Crystals are positively eager to be your friends, and as friends they are superb. They are mellow, forgiving, unjudgmental, affectionate, loyal, cheerful, joyful and wise. If you are looking for true, undemanding, unflagging friendship, simply pick up the closest crystal and hold it while you watch TV or read a book. This will attune you to its vibration, and it to your vibration. Then meditate with the crystal, clearing your mind to sense its thoughts and personality. Or try projecting yourself inside the crystal to feel its totality. If you use the crystal for healing, tune into it while you're working with it. Notice the crystal's absolutely one-pointed concentration as it directs its thought energy into a wounded or imbalanced area.

It generally takes time to fine-tune your telepathic skills and establish rapport with your crystals, but with perseverance you should develop quite a strong sense of crystals as living, intelligent entities with distinctly individual personalities, especially if you are working with the silica-based quartz family. And you can know for certain that these wonderful beings would be honored to be your friend, now and forever. In fact, since crystals are so long-lived, if you have a lot of crystals it is entirely possible that at least one of them is already an old friend from a former lifetime.

MEDITATION FOR HEALING AND TRANSFORMATION

24

Be Sure of Your Inner Guidance

Many people have asked me how they can be certain that all of the psychic information they get is really coming from their true spiritual guides. This is a vital topic, because the highest and best information available to us is always that which is encountered on the finer planes. So it behooves us all to keep in constant close touch with our inner guidance, but . . . we must all be very certain where this guidance is coming from.

In the world of nature, tiny kangaroo embryos must make their way alone from the birth canal all the way up to the safety of the mother's pouch, and the journey is not without risk. Working with our psychic senses is much the same; for a while at the very beginning we are somewhat on our own while we work to raise our vibrations to a safe level where we can see or sense precisely where our information is coming from. In the meantime, here is the dilemma: Should we trust all of the information our psychic senses relay to us, some of it, or none of it?

Many extraordinary Angels and other healers, Masters, and guides from all over the Universe are working with us from the finer planes. These wonderful people are ready, willing and able to be of service to us as we carry out our healing service to others. Unfortunately, there is also a large, rowdy number of less developed entities dwelling on the lower astral plane who delight in masquerading as guides and Masters. They are fond of intruding on our meditations and giving us their own brand of information, which is frequently erroneous and misleading and sometimes dangerous. They tend to do this during the times when our biorhythms are low and our sensitivities are somewhat dulled. So while 75% of the time we might be perfectly in tune with our spiritual guides, the other 25% of the time we are liable to be receiving some questionable information coming in from impostors on the lower astral frequencies. These frequencies are louder, or more coarse, than the frequencies of the finer levels and are easier to pick up in meditation on a hurried or "off" day.

Following are some examples of situations that have happened to some of our lightworkers. True guides from the highest levels would never do any of the following. If you are getting any of these occurrences, be careful.

1. A "guide" calls you stupid or makes disparaging, negative remarks about you or someone else. Disgraceful!

2. Just as you are falling asleep, a "guide" yells, "Danger!" and then gives no other information. This is typical; by making you nervous so you get a poor night's sleep, fake guides keep you out of tune so you don't detect their deceptions. True guides help ease you into a gentle, restful, peaceful sleep for the physical body and show you ways to be of service on the higher astral planes while you are out of the body at night.

3. Your "guides" start telling you about terrible things that are going to happen to you. *Not!* True guides never discuss major trials that might be coming your way; they always look at the positive side of life. If some heavy circumstance is about to occur, they will quietly prepare you for it, but they will not discuss it with you.

4. Your "guides" play unpleasant tricks on you. Something is definitely wrong here! True guides never engage in sharp or unpleasant humor. Their humor is gentle and is never at the expense of yourself or anyone else.

5. Your "guides" suggest harming or working against another person or living being "for the good of humanity." Never! True guides follow policies of live and let live, nonjudgment and non-violence. Working against another person brings heavy karma back on you and impedes your spiritual development. If you encounter someone negative or evil, simply ignore them.

6. Your "guide" suggests using alcohol or heavy drugs to "tune in better." Just the opposite! True guides work to develop your psychic senses naturally and wholesomely. Drugs and alcohol eventually destroy the chakras and put holes in your auric field, which makes you even more susceptible to lower-astral entities and their poor guidance.

7. Your "guides" suggest practicing extreme austerities such as a prolonged starvation diet. Don't do it! True guides believe in following the middle path. Extreme austerities in this age of violence and pollution only tune you in to unpleasant negative vibrations. Be good to yourself. You have a lot of important work to accomplish and you need the strength and clarity of mind to do so.

8. Either your "guides" speak in lofty, convoluted pseudo-scientific terms that are difficult or impossible to follow, or their control of the language is childish and grammatically atrocious. This is often a scam. Because their primary goal is to communicate with you, true guides speak as clearly as possible. Some quite

reputable guides use quaint speech from other eras, but they use it well, in clear, direct sentences.

If your inner guidance ever has any of the above negative characteristics, pay special attention and use your common sense. When in doubt as to what to do in a difficult situation, wait until a day when you are seeing more clearly. Never do anything that makes you uneasy or goes against your heart or conscience.

Finally, if you don't know who your guides are, ask! If they are taking the time to guide you in a careful and conscientious manner, surely you can go to the trouble of finding out who they are. Reputable guides will be happy to tell you about themselves but will do so in modest terms. If a "guide" brags about how highly placed and powerful he or she is, beware.

In short, our spiritual guides are among our best, dearest and closest friends and their words and actions should *always* confirm that. Your guides and the Masters care for you deeply and they are constantly working for your safety, happiness, and well-being.

25

The Joys of Meditation

It seems that I never get enough time to meditate, and when I do find a few minutes I can't make my mind blank. Too much is going on in my head. How can I get past this and get more out of my meditation? Do I really need to meditate that much in order to be an effective healer?

Z.V., Dallas, Texas

Yes! Meditation is essential for healers if you wish to work on a deep, permanent level. Many people have problems with meditation, and in this day and age — with the overwhelming number of conflicting vibrations that fill the psychic airwaves — such problems are difficult to get past. The purpose of making your mind blank is to shut off the sensations of this world so you can focus on the finer sensations of the astral and mental plans. But since we tend to live in closely packed neighborhoods, the moment we try to clear our minds we are inundated with other people's thoughts, problems, anger, anxieties and so on. It's like trying to hear the soft sound of the breeze over the roar of a raging river. Not an easy task! But it can be done if you have the determination and the desire to do so.

Who Needs Meditation?

Everyone needs meditation! Meditation is life insurance. Rest assured that your efforts to meditate will benefit not only this lifetime but all of your future incarnations. Paramahansa Yogananda said that seven generations of your immediate family will also benefit from the energy that you receive and create in meditation. In addition, deep meditation brings huge floods of high-vibrational energy down into the Earth's aura where it is of benefit to all who need it, including the Earth herself and her flora and fauna.

Would You Like to Swing on a Star? Carry Moonbeams Home in a Jar?

Meditation is endlessly fascinating. How would you like to spend an afternoon seeing your past-life adventures; exploring the fabulous crystalline structures of Atlantis; visiting a rainbow-hued healing temple on Venus; sitting in a fragrant garden at the feet of a Spiritual Master; watching silvery Angels high above an emerald green sea; or looking into a magical sphere that foretells the probable future of the Universe? Meditation can easily take you to all of these places. And you don't need to buy plane tickets, pack clothes, pay hotel bills or find parking places. You just close your eyes and go, here and now.

Meditation is deeply fulfilling. Are you ever lonely? Do you have questions no one can answer? Or do you have difficulty finding words to express your innermost feelings, needs, wishes, desires? Meditation is like logging on to a computer bulletin board . . . all of a sudden you're in potential contact with millions of highly evolved souls from all over the Universe. They have a vast array of interests and skills and they all communicate via telepathy, which bypasses words altogether. Think a thought and the person receiving it will understand perfectly every nuance, memory and reference connected with the thought. Get to know people on levels you never imagined were possible, and know that they understand precisely what you're going through and where you're coming from.

Meditation is healing. No matter how hard life gets, no matter how low you go, in meditation you can shrug off physical difficulties as easily as a bird takes flight. Once you gain altitude you can look at your problems from an entirely different perspective, gaining divine insight as to the true nature and origin of any difficulty. In meditation you can consult with various specialists of great wisdom and experience who are ready and willing to help you and your family, friends and clients with their thoughtful insights and suggestions.

Meditation is divine. Some people envision the Divine Power as a grey-bearded man in robes or as being Buddha-like, Christ-like or whatever. Meditation will show you God in the form of a chipmunk, a bird, a crystal, a tree, a mountain, a lake, a star. Meditation will show you God as an ever-changing panorama of souls, flowing endlessly throughout all of infinity. But meditation will also show you your own personal, much-beloved and long-forgotten face of God in the form that is the most delicious to you — male or female, young or old, brown, red, black, yellow or white. Do you need a parent, a child, a friend, a helper, a lover or a protector? The Divine is all of these to you. The Divine is your true twin soul — your other half — your closest companion throughout eternity, manifesting in one especially beloved form that is just for you and no one else. Meditation is the way to reach out and touch this familiar, sweet face of God.

Meditation is bliss. When you come out of meditation, is your shirt wet with tears of pure joy? It can be. Meditation can fill your soul with a nectar that leaves you soaring for days, months and years. This nectar then begins to permeate your physical life as well. Worries fall away, friendships seem to deepen, the body becomes stronger, work becomes play, and play becomes an expression of sheer exuberance. No matter what the weather, it always feels like spring inside your mind. It's the giddy, ever-exciting experience of being in love on a divine scale, and it fills every moment of your existence.

Get a Life! An Inner Life!

Why limit yourself to the vague, disappointing inconsistencies of this physical dimension? Just because your physical body is stuck on Earth doesn't mean your mind and spirit have to lie low too. Meditation can give you anything your heart desires. You can project your mind and soul into many places, into many times, into many dimensions. It doesn't matter if your physical body is shackled in the deepest, darkest dungeon without a ray of sunshine . . . you can still learn to release your spirit into the absolute freedom of unlimited Divine Light. This is the virtual reality of the mind.

Meditation requires at least twenty minutes a day. It's true that it's not always easy to meditate: it requires patience and perseverance. Some days are frustrating, some days are scrambled, some days are just "off." But the rewards for making the effort are so stupendous that there is simply nothing else on the planet that even remotely compares to it. So why not seriously try it? Have you got anything better to do than to strive for bliss? Your first attempts may be tentative and faltering, but with steady effort can you dare imagine how far you could be in a year, or in five, ten, or twenty years? As the Chinese say, a journey of one thousand miles starts with a single step.

Stay Tuned . . .

In the next few chapters we will discuss some angelic meditation methods that are relatively easy to use, even in this hectic twentieth century. They're fun, almost anyone can do them, and with practice they will bring you a wealth of very exciting experience and knowledge. Try deep meditation, you'll like it!

26

The Angel's Master Meditation Technique

In the previous chapter we discussed some of the reasons why meditation is so vital to our physical, emotional, mental and spiritual well-being. Now let's roll up our sleeves and explore some of the specific meditation techniques that can bring your inner goals within reach.

First Things First

The first thing you need in order to meditate successfully is the desire to do so and a very firm commitment. The mind is like a muscle . . . in order to build it up and get it trimmed down and ready for action, you must work at it steadily. If you were exercising your body, would you go to the gym only six times a year and expect to see noticeable results? No way! The same is true of meditation. As you meditate, you begin to raise the vibrations of your spinal energies, which in turn affect every part of your physical and subtle bodies. But if you meditate only sporadically, you lose the energy impetus that each meditation session produces. So if you want good, lasting results, decide up front that you will make a good, lasting effort. Just meditating on weekends won't get you very far, so plan to set aside twenty to thirty minutes every day for meditation. Remember, we're not talking about drudgery here — we're talking about high energy and high adventure! We're talking about fun! So make some time for it . . . you won't regret it.

The second thing you need is a quiet place free from distractions such as children, pets, phones, TV, radios, loud traffic and so on. I know it's not always easy to get away from it all, and you might find that early in the morning or late at night is the best time to meditate. It's important to pick a time when you are alert and focused, so if you are a morning person meditate early rather than at night, and if you are a night person meditate at night rather than in the morning. It helps if you meditate at the same time every day and it is also important to meditate in the same place every day; this quickly builds very strong vibrations into your meditation place, which will tend to magnetically pull you deeply into meditation as soon as you sit down to begin. If possible, a few pictures of Spiritual Masters or perhaps a photo of an inspiring landscape such as one of India, Egypt, Greece, Stonehenge, the ocean, or dolphins will help build a special vibration into your meditation space. Soothing music can also be helpful and earphones are especially useful if there is a lot of noise outside.

The third thing you need is loose, comfortable clothing. Cotton and silk are preferable because they do not interfere with the chakras. If you sit to meditate, a comfortable chair, a pillow or a backsupport also helps. Some of you will find it more restful to lie down as you meditate; this holds your spine straight with the least amount of effort. A full lotus is nice if you can easily achieve it, but if you can't, don't worry about it. Bliss does not depend on your ability to pretzel yourself!

The fourth thing you need is something to boost the energy of your chakras. If you work with Power Tools, enough said . . . use whichever ones you have, most especially the third-eye disks. Otherwise, use crystals and/or gems on your third eye and on any other chakra that seems low in energy. The easiest way to use crystals and Power Tools is to lie down and place them on your chakras the whole time you meditate or hold them to your chakras for five or ten minutes prior to meditation.

The next thing you need is a good, reliable spiritual guide. Most of you are probably already working with guides, but if you are not, I suggest watching for the Angels in meditation or for the Divine Mother. The Angels are beautiful, delightful, humorous, helpful, knowledgeable and very, very good at what they do. The Divine Mother is quite simply your very best friend, whether you remember it or not, and she has been close to you for every one of your lifetimes. She is also a Spiritual Master of breathtaking abilities. So if you don't have a guide and you want to be dazzled now and forever, opt for an Angel or for the Divine Mother, or both.

Finally you need meditation techniques that can get you where you wish to go. We will discuss techniques in detail for the next few chapters, starting here and now with a basic technique that will give you altitude and raise your vibrations; then we will follow up with a fabulous technique for exploring yourself in the context of who you were before you came to Earth, and for looking into some of the special things you have done since you incarnated here.

The Master Technique

I've written about this technique at least twice before, but I will repeat it here because it is so very important, so very useful and so very effective. Although it takes only four or five minutes, it will raise your spinal energies beautifully and flood your cerebral meditation centers with pure psychic force. If you're already using this technique, please skim through it again to be sure you're doing it correctly.

To begin, lie down with a crystal or Power Tool on your forehead over the third eye (and on other chakras if you like) or sit so you can comfortably hold the crystal or Power Tool in place. Breathe deeply and slowly through your solar plexus for about two minutes. This will prepare you for deep meditation by pulling large amounts of soul energy down into your physical body.

Next, visualize or form a strong, clear idea that you are rising up out of your physical body in a body made of pure, rich gold light. When you are standing up in this gold body, visualize the physical landscape fading away and in its place a beautiful green meadow beginning to shimmer and take form. Fill in grass, flowers, trees, sky, birds and so on. Notice that in the center of the meadow is a large pyramid made of brilliant white light. It has steps going up all four sides, leading to a capstone of gold light. This pyramid is about sixty feet tall, with the capstone comprising the top ten feet. Visualize youself walking over to the pyramid in your gold body and standing by the first step.

The point of this meditation technique is to climb the pyramid; as you climb, energy will begin to flow up your spinal column from the first (base) chakra all the way to the crown of your head. This is like raising an antenna on a radio to prepare it to receive incoming sound waves — only in this case, you're preparing to receive incoming thought waves and spiritual vibrations.

As you begin to climb, focus on your gold legs and take high steps. Almost immediately you should get the sensation of rising: this tells you that the energy is beginning to flow up your spine. Climb 64 steps straight up; with the 64th step, enter into the gold light of the capstone.

Sit down and make yourself comfortable. Let the gold light of the capstone flow through your gold body, filling it with intense energy. You should have a feeling of having climbed to an enormous height. Now take a moment to visualize an eye that fills your whole mind. This opens your third eye and prepares it for meditation.

From here you can do whatever you wish. If you know other meditation techniques, you will find that they are more profound from the top of the pyramid because you have, in effect, put your antenna up. If you don't know any other meditation techniques, try some of the methods we will discuss in the next chapters. *Just remember that when you are done with your day's meditation you should always climb back down the pyramid and bring your gold body back inside your physical body.* This will not only keep you from burning out your psychic centers, but it will also help you bring any information you have gathered during your meditation back down to the physical level where you can remember it and use it.

It's also a good idea to take notes immediately after a meditation session, because the whole process is cumulative. You may see bits and pieces of things today that won't fall into place until two months or two years down the road, so write down anything that seems intriguing or important.

If you are a professional healer, you will discover that this basic technique and the ones to follow will add tremendously effective new dimensions to your healing work. First, they will tune you in very well, and second, they can be used on your clients to help them see the roots of their strengths, weaknesses, traumas and so on. Just put a few crystals or Power Tools on their chakras, especially the third eye, and lead them up the pyramid. Most people have no difficulty seeing all sorts of things quickly and easily. When you're finished with the session, be sure to lead them back down the pyramid and return them to their physical bodies.

The Magical Suitcase

It's important to remember that you are much more than this one incarnation; your soul has been around forever, with never a dull moment. So it's extremely helpful and enlightening to put yourself into the context of at least your earth round of incarnations. The suitcase technique will help you do that.

As you sit in the capstone of your pyramid, visualize that you have with you an interesting-looking suitcase, or a knapsack, overnight bag, or whatever. Inside this suitcase are important mementos of your earth lives as well as a few precious reminders of your life before you came to this planet. The meditation technique consists of simply opening your suitcase and rummaging around, seeing what memories you have considered important enough to save. Everyone has different experiences and memories, so I'll tell you some of the things I found in my suitcase. Yours will be similar in some ways and different in others.

You will undoubtedly come across several small photo albums with about ten to twenty photos each showing highlights of various past lives. For example, some of the albums I found were marked Angelic Kingdom, Pleiades, Andromeda, Lemuria, Atlantis, Egypt, Greece, India, Tibet and Scotland. In the Lemurian album so far I have found just one photo, of myself traveling rapidly from north to south as the continent was breaking up into a smoldering mass. Inside the Egyptian album I found a photo of the rural area where I was born, one of my family, a few photos of the temple where I served, several of the people who were dear to me, and about five snapshots that triggered memories of certain major events. As you examine the pictures a lot of information and emotions will come sweeping over you . . . it's very trippy, mostly fun, but can contain some trauma.

Next, I found a bunch of gold hearts about the size of the palm of my hand. Each heart opened up to reveal the face of a loved one from my past lives. There were many beloved faces of people I have incarnated with often, and there were several faces of guides and friends from my home world before I came to Earth.

A little black book with medical records appeared next, tracing certain problems I'm having in this life back to different incarnations, some as far back as Atlantis. Some of these things were not fun to remember, but they cleared up a lot of mysteries and alleviated many symptoms.

Then there were a bunch of personally significant miscellaneous things: an other-worldly ring from my twin soul, two violins from the Angelic Kingdom, a wooden bowl and a coin from India, a crystal tool from Atlantis, five scarabs and a sacred papyrus scroll from Egypt, a book of schematics for the Power Tools I agreed to bring to this planet — and there was even a little bundle of recipes of favorite dishes that can easily be made in this day and age. It's very interesting to eat these things again, and healthful too, since the foods are basic and simple.

These are just a few of the many, many things I have found in my suitcase over the past few years. You will find that your suitcase is pretty much bottomless. There are always more treasures to find, more memories, more associations, more friends and more interesting events to remember. You are also likely to find an accumulation of special insights and techniques that will help you evolve and grow spiritually; these have probably come from initiations you have undergone.

Above all, have fun with this technique and use it often. Over a period of several months or years you will find that it is a real gold mine of priceless memories and valuable information.

27

Several Auxiliary
Meditation Techniques

In the last chapter we discussed an excellent basic technique for raising the kundalini in order to inundate the psychic centers with energy. This chapter will add to your meditation skills using the same Master Technique and then building on it. All of the following techniques are used *after* you have entered your gold body and climbed the pyramid. A crystal or a Power Tool held up to your third eye for five or ten minutes will increase your results significantly.

You will find that as you begin to meditate regularly you will feel better, have more energy, find simple solutions to complex problems, come into a state of wonderful emotional balance, and enjoy a heightened clarity of thought. If you are a professional healer you will be more tuned in to your clients and if you, in turn, help them to meditate, they will heal much faster and be happier campers.

After the Master Meditation:
Finding Your Special Place

Everyone has seen the classic image of the Buddha meditating under his tree. You too can have a marvelous private meditation space where you go as soon as you climb your pyramid. The trick is to have your spot on the finer planes rather than in the physical dimension.

From the top of your pyramid begin to imagine taking shape all around you a special place that represents your absolutely ideal landscape. It could be a garden filled with spring flowers, roses, fruit trees, bird songs and a little fish pond. It could be a hidden grotto with exotic plants. It could be on the top of a high, high mountain. It could be inside a cave filled with crystals, it could be in a majestic forest, it could be on the beach by a serene ocean, it could be in a dome under the sea. It could be on a beautiful distant planet. It could be just about anywhere, so long as it seems wonderful to you.

Spend a lot of time imagining this ideal place. Picture its basic details at the beginning of your meditation each day, making the image more elaborate with every session. Try going through garden catalogs looking for lovely plants for your special place, and don't forget shade and fruit trees, small animals such as rabbits, squirrels, chipmunks, butterflies, songbirds and perhaps a few nature spirits. What color is the sky? What is the climate like? Eventually, you can begin to fill in the whole landscape as far as the inner eye can see. If you are good at visualization you can build yourself a large area that you can roam at will. Would you like a little house or a cabin or a tipi? Just fill it in with a great deal of loving detail for each room, wall, table or chair. Above all, have fun with it. Building this place and spending meditation time there should be a source of comfort, joy, relaxation and mellow energy for you.

There are two major possibilities as to what you are accomplishing with this exercise. The first is that as you go over the details of your special place in your meditation each day, the energy and clarity of your thoughts will begin to form precisely such a place for you on the mental plane. Then every time you go there and visualize the surroundings, your place will take on more energy and astral substance until it is very much a true astral hideaway that will in turn energize you every time you go there.

The important thing in this circumstance is to visualize very clearly. The finer planes are chock full of strange imagery formed by careless thoughts — buildings with fronts but no backs, gorgeous rooms with dirt floors, or the trunks of trees with green haze instead of leaves and branches. In fact, it is amusing to note that many people visiting the astral plane at night as their physical bodies sleep remember to manifest clothing but forget about the backs of their bodies; consequently, they look as if they are walking around in hospital gowns with nothing whatsoever on if you happen to see them from behind. So the important thing here is clear detail, which brings strength and longevity into your special space as well as into your other meditations.

A second possibility as to what is happening during this exercise is that as you are shopping around in your mind for an ideal place, landscape images will start to form for you that are from a past life, perhaps from a beloved incarnation on Earth or from your home world before you came here. If this is the case, each time you go to your special place in meditation you will actually be projecting your mental body through time and space to the site of the original location. Sending your mental vehicle to such places on a daily basis greatly benefits your psychic and spiritual energies, helps you remember your greater self, and evolves you much more quickly.

How can you know whether you are forming your own place

from scratch or visiting an old familiar place? Time will usually tell. If you start seeing objects, people, animals or new parts of the landscape that you are not supplying from your own thoughts, chances are you are remembering the site of a former incarnation. For many people, at first it will seem as if the place is forming from your own mind; then suddenly there will be new details, and you will realize that it is a place you have been before, after all. That's part of the adventure of meditation, so just follow it along and see what develops.

Trust me, this is one glorious meditation technique! When you've been doing it for a while you will wonder how you ever survived without it. Also, when your private spot is well established and easy to visualize, try using the suitcase technique described in the previous chapter. You will find that you can keep your suitcase in your special place along with many other things, including items related to the new techniques that follow below and in the next couple of chapters. In short, do all of your meditations from your private spot and you will be coming from a place of amplified personal power. This will put vast quantities of extra energy into your meditations as well as into every other aspect of your life. Above all, enjoy yourself.

The Fortune Cookie

I love this fun little technique. It's very simple. As you sit in your special place, mentally hold out your hand and imagine that a bag of Chinese fortune cookies is materializing in your palm. Open it, choose a cookie and see if you can read your fortune. If you are more clairaudient than clairvoyant you will hear the words rather than see them. Your fortunes will come from your personal guides, the Angels, or the Divine Mother, and they will always be positive; negativity has no place in meditation, as it only undermines our progress. So stash your bag of cookies somewhere in your special place and have a really positive, pertinent fortune cookie every day.

The Treasure Chest

This is similar to the fortune cookie technique. Imagine that a wonderful treasure chest appears before you as you sit in your special place. In it are gifts to you from your guides, the Angels, and the Divine Mother. Each day reach in and pull out one item, then meditate on its significance for you. Again, it will always be something positive. If you see something bizarre, it is only physical-plane interference, so try again. If you get something like a jewel it will probably represent an abstract or complex thought that you might want to work with for a while in order to understand its full significance. When you are finished, find a place to store your treasure chest in your special place so it will be waiting for you the next time you meditate.

The Valentine Box

Remember Valentine's Day in grade school? There was usually a shoe box covered with white, pink, or red paper and cut-out hearts, with a slot in the top. Well, hold out your hands as you sit in your special spot and visualize just such a box. Now mentally open the lid, reach in and take out a valentine. It will be a memory of a loved one from a former incarnation or a message from someone in your present life who has passed on. Again, find a place to store your valentine box. In fact, you might try visualizing a special place to keep all of these items; put them under a tree, on a kitchen table, or whatever.

The Archaeological Expedition

Over in a far corner of your special place is an interesting heap of rocks, rubble and mysterious small items. Imagine that you are an archaeologist. Buried under the rubble are many past-life objects that hold special memories and significance for you. Dig away and see what you can find, then focus on each item to tune in to its meaning and memories. Feel free to visualize a pith helmet for yourself, khaki shorts, shovels, a tent, the whole nine yards. You will be surprised at what you can find with a little perseverance. And of course, all good archaeologists take careful notes.

You will find that all of these meditation techniques — the pyramid, your special place, the suitcase, the bag of fortune cookies, the treasure chest, the valentine box and the archeological site — will get stronger and clearer the more you use the images.

The Bell Meditation

This technique is a bit different from the others because instead of looking for information, the point is to send extra kundalini energy up your spine. Think of kundalini energy as pure life force. If you do this meditation about once a week, you will feel better, your mind will be clearer and your other meditations will be much more exciting.

In order to do this technique you will need two things: a set of earphones (very important) and a tape, record, or CD with the sound of chimes or bells. I've tried all sorts of sounds and I've gotten the best results with Swiss or Hawaiian bells and chimes. Although I have deep roots in Tibet, the Tibetan bells are a bit too slow and low-pitched for me for this meditation. You will have to experiment to see which sounds are best for you. Sometimes xylophone music is excellent for this also . . . you just need something that chimes melodically. If you don't have earphones and don't want to look for music, try buying your own set of chimes.

As you listen to the music, climb your pyramid in your gold body and visualize yourself in your special place. Then begin to focus on the sound of the bells. Imagine that each chime originates in the lower tip of your spine and then flows rapidly and sweetly up your spine, all the way out the top of your head. Ten or fifteen minutes of this will give you a very mellow buzz as your energy begins to rise powerfully.

An alternate method is to let the lower tones originate from the tip of the spine (the base chakra); to visualize that the highest tones originate from the third eye and crown chakras; and to fit the midtones between the higher and lower chakras. Wherever the tone originates, send it up and out of the crown chakra.

If you want more power, assign colors to the chimes: red light for the first chakra, orange for the second, yellow for the navel, white for the solar plexus, green for the heart, blue for the throat, indigo for the third eye and violet for the crown. Or you can simplify things and just visualize one color per session; choose from green, white, pink, violet or gold light.

For some, this will take a bit of practice, but when you manage to get that sound and color zinging up your spine you will be handsomely repaid for your efforts. As they used to say in the '60s, *"Like, wow!"*

Summary

You will find that the short techniques above are fun and greatly rewarding. Most of you will get good results the first or second time you use them. However, it is vitally important to do the basic gold body/pyramid technique very carefully first; then go to your special place. From there your efforts will have much, much more power. And please remember to climb down the pyramid when you are finished and bring your gold body back into the physical. If you don't, you will lose a lot of the energy you accumulated during your meditation, so be sure to bring yourself back down just as carefully as you took yourself up.

28

Advanced Meditation Techniques

The meditation techniques presented in these last chapters are advanced, which means they will take more time and concentration to master. However, if you meditate regularly — and especially if you use Power Tools or crystals — they should be well within your reach.

Be a Book Browser

When I first began to get psychic — and it happened all at once! — the Divine Mother suggested this technique to me, and it has really paid off in my life, big-time. Even though it's an unusual technique, I still use it today. You probably won't get immediate feed-back because the goal is more long-term, but the results you do get are generally awesome and they come just when you need them most.

The first part of the technique is so simple that a child can do it; in fact, children do it all the time and you have probably done a fair share of it yourself. All you have to do is pick up an interesting book in a library or bookstore and fan rapidly through the pages, with concentration, about five times. It takes only about ten or fifteen seconds per book.

The idea is that you are feeding your brain information at subliminal speed. This information will be stored away in its entirety, as everything we see always is, and if you meditate regularly from time to time this information will become available to you when it is necessary or appropriate.

For about six months I skimmed books on a variety of topics: foreign languages, computer languages, history, astronomy, flight and space travel, home building, survival, mathematics, all branches of science, medicine and first aid, cookbooks, complete sets of encyclopedias — whatever seemed useful. It can become quite habit-forming as you look for books to add to your mental library.

When you have skimmed through a fair number of books, you will notice that as you are fanning through the pages you will suddenly begin to see whole phrases and sentences perfectly clearly, even though each page is visible for only a fraction of a second. This phenomenon happens as your brain makes clear photographs of every page and stores the images in your memory banks.

The difficult part of the technique is retrieving the information. With luck you will find that somehow you begin to know things that you don't remember studying. You might hear a scientific definition on a quiz show such as *Jeopardy* and think, "Oh, that must be the definition of an erg." Then you'll think, *"What did I just say?!"* And then Alex Trebek will say, "The answer is, what is an erg?" Similar things can happen in a variety of situations, when knowledge just comes to you out of the blue. And if you stop to think about it, perhaps you will remember skimming a particular book that dealt with the topic in question. It works.

In this life, the information may or may not come to you very often, but consider this: your soul retains a perfect record of every single thing you learn in each incarnation, and when you are out of the body between incarnations or after your round of earth incarnations is finished, that knowledge is generally freely available to you. This means that whatever you take the trouble to skim becomes totally yours sooner or later. So if you wish, you can soak up a great deal of quite useful information for your higher self, and from time to time it will amaze your lower self also.

If, like so many lightworkers, you consider yourself to be visiting this planet from somewhere else, you will immediately see the advantage of gathering vast quantities of information in this simple way. Who knows just how useful it will prove to be if you incarnate on this Earth again or when you return to your home world?

This technique can be boosted considerably if you take a few moments to mentally climb the pyramid in your gold body (as discussed in prior chapters) and anchor yourself in your special place. This will call in higher aspects of your soul and etch the information into a higher level of consciousness.

Be a Coin Collector

This technique is one of my all-time favorites but is an acquired talent and requires a good, concentrated effort. Begin by finding a penny, dime, quarter or silver dollar that is a bit worn out from circulation so you can be certain many people have handled it. Next, hold a quartz crystal or third-eye Power Tool up to your forehead to prepare yourself for deep meditation. Then climb the pyramid in your gold body and go to your special place.

When you are anchored in your special place, hold the coin up to your forehead and imagine that you are walking right into it;

just project your consciousness inside the coin. Then ask to see what the coin has been used to buy, and by whom. You should begin to see all sorts of people who have carried the coin, as well as stores where the coin has been spent and the items the coin has been used to purchase.

This is fascinating in itself and it gives you practice with psychometry, which is the very valuable metaphysical art of psychically reading the history of an object. But if it turns out that you can read your coins easily and clearly, try step two, which is where the real appeal comes in.

To do the advanced exercise, find a coin dealer who deals in ancient coins and contemporary world coins, and buy whatever strikes your fancy. I have a motley collection of contemporary coins from all over the world, but the true prizes of my collection are surprisingly inexpensive ancient coins from Egypt, Greece, Rome, the Byzantine Empire, China, India, Tibet, England, Spain, France and also from an old shipwreck. Can you imagine what it is like to read these coins? You get the whole scenario: a complete nutshell description of the ancient world, including landscapes, sounds, scents, costumes, homes, shops, food, as well as the thoughts of a coin's many owners.

My coins have fascinating historical pictures in them: a wealthy Egyptian lady buying a huge clay water jar in a market, with her slave trailing along behind her collecting her purchases; another Egyptian using the same coin to purchase crocodiles' teeth as a pharmaceutical remedy; a Roman soldier fighting in the army, building bridges, being unfaithful to his wife, and eventually dying of a spear thrust under his armor; a very poor elderly man in China using his little coin (a whole week's wages, worth about a nickel) to buy a wooden bowl and a pair of chopsticks; two road crews in ancient Greece competing to see who could complete its road segment faster; misery and terror in Tibet under the Chinese invasion (for this reason I don't recommend reading Tibetan coins); and a whole slew of other things you can witness precisely as they happened. Not only is it *living history*, but if you were incarnate in one of these places (and you can bet the coins that attract you will be from the sites of former lifetimes), a lot of profound, valuable memories are liable to come up for you also.

And of course, it needn't stop with coins, although their metallic content picks up very strong, clear psychic impressions. Meditation with a piece of mastodon ivory will take you back to the last ice age, and the psychic imprint of the extreme cold will chill you to the very bone. Meditation with a dinosaur fossil will show you the original version of Jurassic Park. A meditative walk through an antique shop holds endless delight. And meditation on something passed down in your family will show you your parents or grandparents from a unique and unexpected perspective.

For healing purposes, once you have learned the basic technique you will find that you can sometimes put your hand over a person's body and read the cause of an illness, and some of you will be able to do the same with just a photograph of a person or something that he or she has held. Or try asking a client to hold a small quartz crystal during a healing session; then psychometrize the crystal as you meditate after the client has gone. You can pick up a lot of very valuable healing insights in this way.

Just a little contemplation will bring to mind many other possibilities that will keep you eagerly reading the past records associated with all sorts of interesting objects in your everyday life. And while you read, you will be fine-tuning your meditation and psychic skills as well as acquiring wonderful insights into a variety of topics.

29

Past-Life Trauma

In order to bring the greatest possible relief to clients, New Age healers must be competent archaeologists. Just as an archaeologist patiently sifts down through the various levels of deposits in a digging site, so healers must slowly and carefully work their way through layer after layer of trauma, negative experiences, and misconceptions in order to ascertain the complex underlying causes of a physical, mental or emotional problem.

For example, let's suppose a client falls off a bicycle and wrenches a knee. The temptation is to believe that the bicycle accident was the entire cause of the problem and that it will be a simple thing to clean up the knee, manipulate it, bandage it, stay off it and let it heal. But frequently such a straightforward injury does not heal either quickly or well; the problem becomes chronic, the knee tends to go out unexpectedly and it worsens with age.

Repeated healing sessions have a short-term effect but fail in the long run. Why?

Nine times out of ten the problem is lodged in the DNA. We all have two kinds of DNA: the temporary DNA that we inherit from our parents and the more permanent DNA that the incarnating soul brings with it into the physical body from the finer planes.

The DNA that you inherit from your parents is primarily concerned with physical characteristics: will your body be tall or short, chubby or slender, with green, blue or brown eyes and so on. In addition, susceptibilities to many diseases and some mental and emotional problems are also carried in the genetic coding, where they are passed down from generation to generation. In short, your physical DNA gives you many of the physical tools and handicaps that you will be working with during each incarnation. As your incarnations change, so do your physical gifts and challenges, allowing you to develop versatility and balance from lifetime to lifetime.

Your spiritual DNA, on the other hand, supplies you with the *living memory* of all of your past-life experiences. Encoded into this DNA are your basic soul characteristics as well as the experiences that have molded your spiritual being.

When the soul enters the embryo of the physical body that is being grown for it, the soul's spiritual DNA patterns are stamped into the physical DNA codes. As the years pass, the two types of DNA interact and modify one another.

Getting back to the bicycle injury, let's say that your client has no susceptibility to a joint problem in his or her physical DNA; why then does it keep recurring? The answer probably lies in the spiritual DNA. If you do a series of past-life regressions with your client, you are liable to find not just one but several instances of knee injury in past incarnations. Perhaps the knee was damaged in a fall in one life, injured in battle during another incarnation and shattered in a rock slide in yet another. The imprint of these injuries is carried from the spiritual DNA into the physical DNA, where it produces susceptibility to yet another injury. So when the client falls off the bicycle, the spiritually weakened knee is likely to be damaged, while other not-so-susceptible body parts escape harm.

Such occurrences happen all the time. We all have things that just won't clear up, and some of them seem to have come right out of nowhere, with no accident or injury to cause the problem. Chronic problems of this type should alert healers; they warrant a careful look into the client's past lives. In cases where the problem simply appears, with no initial accident, something as unlikely as age is sometimes the hidden trigger.

For example, suppose the above battle injury occurred in a past life when the client was twenty three. When the client is twenty-three in this lifetime, the old knee problem is likely to recur. Other unsuspected things can also serve as a trigger: what if the battle injury was caused by a bayonet and the client happens on a bayonet in a museum or sees one in a movie? Such subconscious jolts to past-life memory can also trigger the old knee problem. So it is necessary to ascertain not only what past injuries have occurred and the circumstances of each one, but also the approximate age of the subject at the time of the injury and/or any other possible triggering mechanisms.

It is only when a problem is consciously approached at this depth that it can be permanently cleared and resolved at the soul level. Of course, if the lessons behind the chronic injury still have not been learned, the soul will have to carry the disability through to its conclusion. Even in such cases, however, finding the origin and subsequent recurrences of the injury will always serve as a solid first step toward helping both the healer and the client understand the problem and eventually conquer it.

During the course of a healing session, healers or clients may sometimes catch glimpses of a past-life injury, but all too frequently the deepest origins of a chronic problem will remain cloaked, especially if the client is suppressing the memory through fear or discomfort with the original situation. In such cases it is wise to dedicate at least one hour to past-life regressions so subsequent healing sessions can be conducted in the full light of understanding on the part of both healer and client. No matter what type of healing work you do, whether it is massage, acupuncture, Reiki, crystal work, sound, light, Power Tools, hands-on or what-have-you, you will find that your success rate increases dramatically when it is augmented by past-life work, especially when the client him/herself is able to see the original situation and all of its implications.

30

Beginning the Search
for Past-Life Trauma

he previous chapter discussed the role of past-life trauma as
the root of present-day illness. If you do not know how to
conduct a past-life regression or if your results are not as deep as
you would wish them to be, the following technique will be quite
useful. This method is used in the great angelic healing temples: it
is tried and true and very, very powerful. The first part of the
technique raises the kundalini energy and amplifies the psychic
abilities. The second part (which will be discussed in the next
chapter) deals with accessing specific types of information, including past lives. The technique has been given elsewhere in this
book: it is repeated here in extra detail because it is so vitally
important.

The vibratory plane directly above the astral is the *mental plane,* which is fifth-dimensional in character. This marvelous plane is the storehouse of knowledge and ideas. Here are the master plans for all of the great past, present and future scientific, artistic, musical, philosophic and mathematical works that grace our planet. The Akashic Records of all that has transpired historically on Earth are also imprinted in the superfine energy of the mental plane, where they may be read accurately and relatively easily with just a little practice. In addition, most of the great Masters work on the mental plane, teaching and inspiring those on lower levels. In short, the mental plane is a place of inconceivably important opportunities, and it is well within the reach of almost everyone.

The mental plane is accessed through the mental body. Because we have all been taught mental discipline since childhood, almost everyone has much more control over the mental body than over the astral/emotional body. Furthermore, it is not necessary to leave the physical body in order to access the mental body — it can be easily accessed with the power of your mind.

The following Master Technique is designed to give you conscious control of your mental body. If you first learn and practice the technique yourself, you will find that it will become quite easy to lead clients through the technique as you search for the roots of chronic illness, emotional difficulties and the like, giving your healing work much more depth and finesse.

The technique is done with the eyes closed, generally with crystals or Power Tools on the chakras, or at least on the third eye. As you proceed with the technique, watch carefully in your mind's eye for fleeting images, words or ideas. The images may be faint and fragmentary at first, but with practice they will become clearer, more coherent and much more detailed. If you are primarily clairaudient, words or sentences may form in your mind rather than pictures. Some people will simply find that they suddenly "know" about a situation, without specific words or pictures.

Trust what you see: the information that you get is usually 80% to 95% accurate. It is a good idea to take notes after a session, because the nuances are difficult to remember afterwards and many seemingly random details could prove to be highly significant at some point in the future.

The Master Technique

The Master Technique will raise your vibrations to the point where you can either travel in your mental body or begin to sense things on the mental plane through the eyes and ears of your mental body. There are two major elements of the Master Technique. The first is the Gold Body Visualization, which activates the mental body and moves it away from the physical vehicle. The second element is the Pyramid Visualization, which raises the spinal energies, scans the chakras for problem areas, and opens the third eye. The first time you read through the visualizations they might seem complex, but if you read through them two or three times you will see that they are really quite simple. Because they are so tremendously powerful, it is well worth the effort to learn them.

Step One: The Gold Body

Make yourself comfortable, preferably lying down with crystals or Power Tools on your chakras. Close your eyes and breathe deeply and rhythmically. Breathe pure white light in through the first chakra, pulling it from the front of the chakra back into the spine. Work your way up through every chakra, pulling light through to the spine three or four times at each center. (It's best to count eight chakras: base, second, navel, solar plexus, heart, throat, third eye and crown.) This deep breathing brings bursts of soul energy into the chakras and spine, reinforcing the body's link with the soul and preparing you for deep meditation.

When you have finished with the deep breathing, begin to contemplate what it would be like if your body began to turn into brilliant gold light. Start with your feet and visualize your toes turning into gold light . . . now your ankles . . . calves . . . knees . . . thighs . . . hips . . . torso . . . arms . . . hands . . . neck . . . and head. When you have built a strong image of yourself inside a body of pure dazzling gold light, form a mental picture of yourself standing up in this beautiful body, leaving the physical shell right where it is. You will have now shifted your focus away from the physical body and into the mental body.

Step Two: The Pyramid of Light

As you stand in your gold body, imagine a beautiful meadow beginning to form all around you. Fill in green grass, flowers, trees, birds, sunshine and the like. Visualize right in the center of the meadow a large pyramid made of vibrant white light. Form the pyramid in your mind as clearly as you can. When you visualize something very strongly it will instantly take form in the pliable energy of the mental planes, so by making a clear picture of the pyramid you are bringing it into being for your use in the mental realms. Your pyramid will be just as powerful as your mental image is, so take your time and make the form as sharp and precise as you can. The better it is, the better it will serve you.

The pyramid is large, with steps going up all four sides right up to the capstone, which is made of an exquisite gold light that is even brighter than your gold body. When you have the image of the pyramid clearly in mind, imagine that you are walking over to it in your gold body, getting closer and closer, until you are standing near the base of it. As you approach the pyramid you see that there are eight large, round gems about two inches in diameter set into some of the steps. The first gem is in the very center of the first step; it is a deep ruby red. Eight steps directly above the red stone is a brilliant orange stone; eight steps above that is a bright yellow stone; then a clear, dazzling, diamond-like stone; an emerald-green stone; a shining light blue stone; a mystical deep blue stone; and a gorgeous violet stone. Each gem is eight steps above the preceding stone. Lastly, eight steps above the violet stone the white light part of the pyramid ends and the capstone of gold light begins. The capstone is about ten feet tall; the entire pyramid is about sixty feet high.

You will notice that the colors of the gems match the colors of your chakra system, ranging from the red of the first chakra to the violet of the crown. In fact, the pyramid represents the ascending energy of your spinal column. The gold capstone represents the five chakras above the crown that link to the higher dimensions.

To complete the Master Technique, you have only to climb the pyramid and sit down on top of it inside the capstone of gold light. Although it sound simple, it will accomplish a great deal.

Before you start to climb, focus on the color of the first gem, which is ruby red. Concentrate until you can see a brilliant red in your mind's eye. Then climb the first eight steps and pause until you can visualize the brilliant orange stone. Continue up in this manner, stopping on every eighth step to visualize the color of the gem set into the step; go up past the yellow, clear, green, light blue, deep blue and violet stones. Eight steps above the violet gem step out into the capstone of gold light and pause until you can visualize its sparkling gold color all around you, blending with your gold body.

Now sit down inside the capstone and concentrate until you can conjure up a mental image of a clear, bright, wide-open, alert eye. It will be very realistic and should appear in the center of your mind. When you see it you will have completed the Master Technique and will be ready to meditate deeply, look into past lives, or carry on with whatever else you wish to explore.

Several marvelous auxiliary techniques that can be used at this point will be given in the next chapter, including two specific past-life techniques. In the meantime, the first step is to learn and practice the Master Technique until you are entirely comfortable with it.

What It Accomplishes

Although the Master Technique consists of simply climbing the pyramid eight steps at a time for a total of eight levels and tuning in to a different color at each level, it is much more sophisticated than it seems. Because the colored gems represent your chakras, the colors you see at each level will be the exact colors of your own auric field.

Streaks of gray or black occurring in any color are often an indication of problems within the vicinity of the chakra of the corresponding color. For example, black streaks within the red or orange gem generally indicate either sexual trauma or toxic pollution which is often stored in these two chakras. Grey or black occurring in the green gem can indicate heart problems or emotional difficulties. If you see such dark areas in any chakra, pause and breathe pure white light into the color until the dark regions dissolve and the color becomes brighter. Then proceed to the next level of the pyramid.

If, on the other hand, the color of any gem is clear but faded, this tells you that the energy in the corresponding chakra is low. The crystal or Power Tool you are using on the chakra will usually bring the energy back up to its normal brightness during the course of the session. This will be apparent when you are climbing back down the pyramid.

By the time you have reached the top of the pyramid you will have raised your spinal energy eight full octaves and scanned the condition of every chakra. Because the technique pulls kundalini energy straight up the spine, as you climb you should get an acute sensation of rising to an extreme height. The higher you climb, the more intense the sensation should become. When you notice this feeling, you are doing the technique correctly. (People who do not get the sensation of extreme height or who have difficulty visualizing that they are climbing are likely to have blocks in the flow of spinal energy, which is also useful information.)

By visualizing the gold light of the capstone you will be energizing the five spiritual chakras above the crown. When you form a strong mental image of the eye, you are opening and activating the third-eye center in your mental body. As you sit on top of the structure, the energy the pyramid generates on the mental plane will feed directly into the kundalini region of your mental body, enormously amplifying your psychic abilities.

Getting Back Down

When you have finished with your healing or meditation session, you must bring your energy back down to its normal level. To do this, visualize yourself standing up in your gold body inside the capstone; then begin to climb back down the pyramid eight steps at a time, briefly checking the color at each level. Start with the violet gem and work your way down to the ruby on the bottom step. You should find the colors much brighter than they were on the way up, since your crystals or Power Tools will have energized your system considerably.

After you have reached the bottom of the pyramid, visualize yourself walking over to your physical body and slipping back inside it. Push the energy of your gold hands and feet down into your physical hands and feet, and take several deep breaths to center yourself on the physical plane. Lie still until you feel focused and grounded.

It is very important that you always come back down the pyramid when you have finished your session. If you do not bring your energy down to its normal level you will feel very spacey and unable to concentrate. Your physical coordination will be thrown off as well, and the unusually high energy level in your spine could damage your chakra aystem.

Summary

Gold body . . . pyramid . . . red stone on the first step . . . 8 steps up to the orange stone . . . 8 steps to the yellow stone . . . 8 steps to the clear stone . . . 8 steps to the green stone . . . 8 steps to the light blue stone . . . 8 steps to the deep blue stone . . . 8 steps to the violet stone . . . 8 steps up and into the gold capstone. Sit, visualize the eye. Continue with whichever specific task you have in mind, then climb back down and return to the physical body.

Auxiliary techniques to use from the top of the pyramid, including past lives, past talents, past relationships, blocks, tension release, centering, twin souls, heart links and more will be covered in subsequent chapters. But first, learn the Master Technique, which is the basis for all of the auxiliary techniques. It will make a vast difference in your life!

31

Seeing Past Lives

In the last chapter we discussed a meditation technique from the great angelic healing temples; in the next few chapters we will discuss several auxiliary techniques that can be used in conjunction with the Master Technique. Everyone — especially professional healers — can benefit from these simple but profound methods.

Since past-life information is so vitally important with regard to understanding current-life problems, let's begin with an excellent past-life technique and several variations.

Delving into the Past

Seeing past lives is much easier than most people think. They are, after all, what has molded our present personality as well as our current-life situation. Most peoples' past memories are just beneath the surface of their consciousness, waiting to be released. Many of us discover that certain episodes from past lives have entered into our dreams and have been part of our sleep life for many years. Whether you are looking into the past for your own personal knowledge or doing healing work with another, past-life information is the key to understanding the soul's hopes, passions, fears, illnesses and burdens.

Begin by using the Master Technique: focus your consciousness in your golden mental body, climb to the top of the pyramid of light and sit down in the capstone. Breathe deeply and rhythmically through the solar plexus, heart, throat, third eye and crown chakras. If you have no particular lifetime that you wish to inquire about, ask for information on whatever past incarnation is the most pertinent to you at this time. Ask which country this particular lifetime occurred in, then sit quietly on top of the pyramid of light, watching and listening until the name of a country appears in your mind. It may come immediately or it may take a while, but it will come. Now ask for a date and wait until one appears. It might be general such as 1700 or it might he specific, giving you the exact year you are about to tune in to, perhaps when something major occurred in that particular pastlife. Try to ascertain whether the date is A.D. or B.C. If you are looking for a particular incarnation — for example, one spent in Egypt — then concentrate on Egypt to begin with and ask for the general date of your life there.

Now ask to see a landscape from the lifetime you are working on. Watch for glimpses of trees, plains, desert, ocean, lake, mountains, town, city, or whatever. When you have a picture, no matter how fleeting or faint, visualize yourself standing in the middle of that scenery. Now look up at the sky: is it sunny, cloudy or stormy? If it is bright and sunny, chances are excellent that this is a pleasant incarnation. Memories of clouds generally indicate conflicts, whereas scenes of dark, stormy weather frequently indicate a traumatic lifetime. A stormy past life often holds the keys to major present-life illness and karma. Although it can be unpleasant to review such a lifetime, it is always profoundly illuminating.

For the time being, let's assume that you see a bright, clear sky. The next thing to do is to look down at yourself as you stand in the middle of the landscape and notice if you are male or female, young or old. How are you dressed? Look at your shoes, jewelry, hat and the like: these accessories can give you clues as to whether you were wealthy, poor or middle class. Sometimes an object held in the hands can reveal an occupation,

Next, ask to see the most important building where you lived. You may catch glimpses of several places, but one should be clearer than the rest. Find the door and walk inside. What do you see? How is this place furnished? Where did you sit, eat, sleep? Ask if you lived with anyone, then watch the door to see who walks in. Focus on each person in turn and ask if he/she is anyone you know in your present life.

From this point, continue with questions until you glean all the information you would like to have. Some important things to ask about include childhood, parents, siblings, friends, marriage, offspring, career, major events, goals, accomplishments, personal difficulties, illnesses, trauma, lessons learned, and the cause of death. If you are leading a client on a regression, a small mellow chime sounded after each question will greatly help your client to see the required information: the chime serves as a cue for the superconscious mind to supply each memory.

After you have finished with the lifetime, focus yourself back on the pyramid. If you wish, you may then investigate another incarnation, but you should always bring your gold body back to the pyramid between incarnations.

The first time you tune in to a particular life the details may be sketchy and erratic. If this is the case, try again two or three weeks later. You are likely to find that many more memories are now ready to come through. The first attempt often unlocks the door, so to speak, and subsequent attempts will open the door wider and wider.

Past-life Relationships: In order to trace the past-life relation-ship or karma between yourself (or your client) and another person, ask to see the earliest incarnation you both had together. Then use the above past-life technique to establish a general idea of the events of the lifetime in question; find out the country and approximate date and take a look at the sky. After you have seen your general situation, ask to see the other person as he or she was then; ask to see yourself; ask what the relationship between you was; look for major events between the two of you; find out what lessons you were working on together and what the outcome was; and trace both of your lives in a general way until you each left the body at the end of the incarnation. Then move on to the next major lifetime spent together and so on, up to the present. (This may take several sessions.) Last, find out what lessons each of you is working on in this life and why you have come together again. If you or your client is very tuned in, it is frequently possible to trace a relationship back to lifetimes together on other planets or in other dimensions.

Past-Life Talents: An amazing amount of specific informa-tion can be retrieved from past lives. With a little concentration and effort, skills learned in the past can be useful to you again in this life, especially if they are of a spiritual or metaphysical nature. As with all past-life work, the trick is to ask your superconscious mind the proper questions. Let's consider two examples.

First, suppose you had an incarnation as a healer. Ask ques-tions along the lines of the following: where did you do your healing? How did you heal — with hands, herbs, crystals, elixirs, light, sound? Now ask to see yourself in the place where you did your healing, with the tools of your trade laid out in front of you. Then set up some situation for yourself to heal: imagine, for example, that a man is brought to you with a deep cut in his leg that is bleeding profusely. What would you do for him? Look and see what ideas and images come to you. You will find that you can literally watch your former self heal the man, and what you learn about your techniques may astonish you.

Next you might imagine that you are helping a woman with a difficult childbirth, or a mentally disturbed person, or a person with a high fever, or any other situation that comes to mind. If you yourself have physical problems in your current lifetime, you can sometimes receive some clues as to how to help yourself by looking at how you would have dealt with a patient experiencing such difficulties in your past life. Ask question after question until you have mined all the information you need. It may take several sessions to retrieve it all, but such knowledge can be invaluable.

As a second example, let's assume you have found a past life where you worked with herbs. Ask the following type of questions: What were your most reliable or favorite plants? Ask to see the first one; note its name, size, shape, color of the leaves, flowers and roots. Ask to see where it grew, which month it was harvested, which portions were used, how it was stored, how it was prepared, how it was prescribed, how it was taken by the patient and for how long. Then ask to see a second herb, and so on.

You can use these techniques to recall any kind of information, whatever your past talents might have been. Just be patient, take your time, keep trying, take notes, and ask as many pertinent questions as you can.

Past-Life Origins of Present-Life Illness: For those who have a troublesome chronic illness or a deep-seated phobia in this life and wish to know if it has past-life connections, such a thing can generally be learned. From the top of the pyramid, ask to see any lifetime that has a bearing on the current problem. As above, find out the country, date and your personal situation in the past life that comes to you. Then ask to see the particular event that has led to the current illness. Ask to see it from a distance or on a TV screen, as if it were only a movie, because it is liable to be unpleasant. When you have pieced together the events as they occurred, ask to see why your soul drew this lesson to itself; what it hoped to learn or accomplish because of the event; whether the soul was clearing any old karma; and whether the karma is finished. Then see if you can find out what triggers the old problem in this current lifetime. Is it something visual, such as the memory of a riding accident being triggered by the sight of a horse? Or maybe the trigger is something emotional. Ask your higher guidance how this triggering can be avoided and any other information that might be helpful in clearing up the problem.

Please note: If you (or a client) draw a total, uncomfortable blank when looking for past-life difficulties, it is possible that either the event is too traumatic to be seen at this time, or it will surface later in the dream state. If you suspect some type of deep trauma, tread very carefully. If the trauma is ready to be encountered, it will generally appear rather easily, with very little encouragement. But if you (or your client) can see only black during a search for past-life problems, the trauma is likely to be deep and serious. This is not the same as just drawing a blank: it is a heavy darkness, generally accompanied by feelings of foreboding and terror. If you encounter such a situation while doing a regression on yourself, get professional help. If you are a professional and encounter the problem while working on someone else, proceed with extreme caution and never force the issue.

The Divine Hand

This is a wonderful technique to use after encountering past-life problems, or in any other instance of physical, emotional, mental or spiritual affliction. It is good any time, any place, and is especially helpful when used in conjunction with the Master Technique. However, even those who are in pain and cannot concentrate on the Master Technique will find the Divine Hand Technique to be very helpful all by itself.

From the top of the pyramid, clear your mind of all thoughts and worries and begin to think of whichever Master you hold in spiritual esteem, be it Christ, Krishna, Buddha, Mohammed, Yogananda, Sai Baba, Babaji, St. Germain or any other Great One. Calling on the Divine Mother or the Angels is exceptionally powerful. A strong thought instantly attracts the loving attention of the Master concerned, and you have only to focus on the divine presence. Those who cannot concentrate well enough to see the Master should try to feel his or her comforting vibration. Next, visualize the Master reaching out a hand and touching you. The touch may come over the problem area or on the forehead, the crown or the heart. In any case, if you concentrate as best you can, you should be able to feel the touch or the deep peace that comes from such contact. Feel the touch as long as you can — it can be blissful. The more frequently you use this technique, the more you will benefit from it.

Remember . . .

When you have finished with these auxiliary techniques, always climb down the pyramid and bring the gold body back into the physical. After looking into past-life injuries you are liable to notice a dramatic change for the better in the chakra color of problem areas as you climb back down the pyramid. Also, two or three days after such a session you are liable to feel a rush of exhilaration as you let go of past-life problems and begin to clear them out of your current life.

32

Finding Your Twin Soul

In the last chapter we discussed past-life techniques from the Angelic healing temples; now we will discuss several more auxiliary techniques that can be used in conjunction with the Master Technique. Everyone — and most especially professional healers — can benefit from these simple but profound methods.

Using the following techniques for twin souls and heart links, professional healers can offer special sessions for two people; friends and lovers can use them on their own; and everyone can begin the exciting search for the Divine Beloved (twin soul).

Twin Souls

Everyone has a twin soul. Generally twin souls first appear in your dreams, either during astral meetings or as surfacing soul memories. The experience is tender and blissful, accompanied by a sense of deep yearning. In such astral encounters you can expect a poignant kiss that you will long remember, but twin souls do not generally engage in sex within this planet's astral vibratory realm because there is too much negativity there. No matter . . . a kiss from a twin soul will exceed your deepest expectations and leave you reeling for days. If you have already had such an experience, it is probable that someone out there is looking for you, needing your love and support.

From the top of your pyramid of light, sit quietly with your right hand over your heart and begin to concentrate on feeling your heartbeat. Then hold the base of a clear quartz crystal to your heart chakra so the crystal's point is aiming away from your body. Now visualize that every beat of your heart is flowing through the crystal outward in waves of concentric circles. This should resemble the ripples that spread over the surface of a pond when a stone is dropped into the water. Picture these waves expanding until they pulsate throughout the entire Earth, and then imagine them spreading through the solar system, the universe, and beyond, until they flow throughout all of infinity. (Looking at a map of our universe greatly helps with this visualization.) Take your time and concentrate deeply on sending strong pulses of light out with every heartbeat. The light may be white, rose, gold, violet or rainbow-hued. For an extremely sensitive and gentle vibration, the Pink Rose Power Tool may be used at the heart instead of or in addition to the crystal.

Next, mentally scan these light waves as they travel outward, as if you were looking for a blip on a radar screen. Look in all directions to see if the waves encounter a presence, an energy, or the light of a familiar consciousness. This may happen immediately or it may take days, weeks or months of searching. No matter how long it takes, it is well worth the time invested and you can rest assured that your energy is definitely reaching your twin soul. If both of your psychic systems are intact, you should eventually achieve a communication link.

When you begin to sense a response, no matter how faint, send back quantities of love and warmth. Follow up with mental pictures of yourself and your situation in life. If you feel a quickening of emotion beaming toward you, reply in kind. Twin souls are generally deeply traumatized by the separation between them, so gentleness and softness are welcomed by both.

Each soul has its own keynote, and when you tune in to the note of your twin soul, sooner or later there will come an overwhelming deluge of emotion. Go with the tides — make contact as often as possible, send love and information whenever you have a private moment, and always hold the image of that loved one safely within your heart center. Know that you will come together again precisely when the time is right . . . and let every day between now and then be a time of preparation for that sweet, electrifying reunion.

Living with Your Twin Soul

Until you and your twin soul can be totally reunited, you can still have much of the romance and excitement of living together. After sending energy to your twin soul from the top of the pyramid of light, spend some time visualizing an ideal dwelling: it could be a snug little cabin in the woods, a tipi or a tent, or even a mansion. Imagine where all the rooms are and what they look like and what the ideal landscape outside would look like. Now visualize that you and your twin soul are moving into this place together, materializing furniture, paintings, sculptures, whatever. Visualize that this is a special hideaway for the two of you that no one else knows about, where you can meet whenever you both can find the time to make telepathic contact.

Chances are that the dwelling will evolve into an exact duplicate of someplace you and your twin soul have shared in a past life. By letting these images develop, you will be reinforcing the past ties between you and your twin soul, stirring up old happy memories, and tuning your vibration to the higher planes, which is where the home probably exists. In short, you will be mentally meeting in an old, well-loved place or perhaps your permanent residence on the finer planes, using the familiar vibrations and memories to help reestablish your relationship.

Make this home a place of perfect love and serenity. Visualize yourself there with your twin soul, relaxing, playing, talking together, perhaps gardening or exploring the surrounding area. Even if you can't get a visual picture of your twin soul, keep imagining how it might be — the thoughts will go directly to her or him whether you are aware of the contact or not. Sometimes it takes a lot of thought energy to awaken the twin inwardly. The more thoughts you send out from your special place, the more the energy will magnetize your twin soul, pulling her or his thoughts to the higher vibrational sphere where you can meet telepathically in the peace and solitude required by such an intense relationship.

You will find that you can leave things to surprise one another — perhaps a vase of flowers, a note under a pillow, or a new little tree planted in the yard. These things will be faithfully reproduced in the energy of the finer planes. Then if your twin soul comes mentally to the house and you are not there, he or she will still be likely to find the new little mementos, just as if you were living together here on Earth.

In this way you can not only create an ideal retreat on the finer planes that you can visit mentally at any time, but you will also be strengthening the eternal bond between you and your twin soul in preparation for your next overwhelming reunion.

Heart Links

This technique can be used by any two people who love each other on this plane. It is ideal for parents and children, friends, married couples and the like. Begin with both parties sitting facing each other, each with a crystal in the right hand. When you have climbed the pyramid of light together in meditation, each of you then reaches out and holds your crystal over the heart of the other person, letting whatever feelings you have for that person flow out from your heart, down your right arm, through the crystal and into the other person's heart chakra. After ten minutes or so of this, switch the crystal to your left hand and again hold it over the other person's heart chakra, concentrating on receiving emotions from the other person. Just sit quietly and be open to whatever impressions come to you. Both can send, both can receive, or one can send while the other receives. This is a wonderful way to explore a friendship or to bring new dimensions into a relationship.

Remember . . .

When you have finished with the auxiliary techniques, always climb down the pyramid and bring the gold body back into the physical. After the above techniques you are liable to notice a dramatic change in the colors of the heart chakra as you climb back down the pyramid. Also, for several days after such a session you are liable to feel a strong, pleasant rush of exhilaration.

33

Three Useful Meditations

In the last chapter we discussed twin soul techniques from the angelic healing temples. In this chapter we will discuss several more auxiliary techniques that can be used in conjunction with the Master Technique.

Dealing with Blocks

Frequently, present-day blocks and unnatural fears are the result of past-life trauma. If you or any of your clients have a seemingly irrational terror with no inkling as to why, or if you habitually reach a certain point in meditation and then inexplicably shut down, it is probable that something from the past is blocking you. In such cases one of the following techniques can usually help. However, *a block should never be forced,* because blocks exist to protect the fragile personality from something it is not yet able to cope with. If a block is ready to fall, the following methods will give it the opportunity it needs. If it is not ready to be released, it is wise to let it go until another time. If you are not a professional healer and you suspect something extremely unpleasant is about to be released, you should consider seeking professional help.

The Stone Wall: From the top of your pyramid imagine as clearly as you can a high wall made out of large, square stone blocks. The symbolism here is easy: a stone block stands for a psychological block. Mentally scan the wall until you see one key block that seems to stand out from the rest. Perhaps it will be darker than the others, or larger, or more irregular. Ask your guides for help in breaking up the block, and begin to picture a laser beam of intense white light disintegrating the block into tiny bits. Now look through the hole in the wall resulting from the removal of the key stone. Ask to see what past-life circumstance is behind the block. Ask what country it relates to . . . the date . . . ask to see yourself as you were then . . . the situation that caused the problem . . . how it affects your life today . . . and what triggers the problem.

If you begin to feel uneasy, cloak yourself in pure white light and remember that the wall is between you and the event, and that you are separated from the situation by a great deal of time. When you have gathered the information you need, visualize that you are filling in the gap left by the block with brilliant light, weaving it into clear glass or crystal. Ask your guides for help with this, and watch the light intensify until the area is intact, clear, and bright. Do this with every block you can find, but don't tax yourself too much on any one day. It's best to spread this kind of work out over a period of weeks or months.

Doors: This is the same technique as above, only instead of a stone wall, visualize that you have the key to a door that has been locked for a long time. Approach the door, cloak yourself in white light, open the door and look. Ask the same questions as given above. Finish up by filling the doorway in with white light, then turning it into a clear doorway of glass or crystal. This still provides a separation between you and the event (there's no need to constantly relive it; seeing it once is enough) but keeps the situation from recamouflaging itself.

The TV Set: If you encounter a stubborn block that you feel is trying to clear but the above methods don't show you the problem, try visualizing a little TV set in the center of your mind. Picture yourself pulling up the TV's antenna, turning the set on and watching the screen fill up with light. Turn the channel indicator until you encounter a clear picture of the situation that caused the block. Fiddle with the focus until you get to the roots of it. Those who are clairaudient can picture a little radio instead of a TV set. Just turn it on, adjust the antenna and turn the station dial until you get a news blurb of the event. Listen for the time, place, cause and so forth.

One Pertinent Question: If all else fails, ask yourself a simple question: What type of current news event makes you the most uneasy? What type of thing sets your teeth on edge each and every time you hear it reported on TV or read about it in the paper? Is it war, famine, flood, fire, torture, kidnapping, child abuse, murder, rape? This will give you a clue as to what you are probably up against. At this point professional help is your best bet. If you are a professional healer, you can then retry one of the above techniques. Please remember, however: Blocks should never, ever be forced. If a block refuses to show itself through the above techniques, it is still serving a purpose and is not yet ready to be cleared. Rest assured that when the time and circumstances (and perhaps karma) are right, it will happen.

Life Force

From the top of your pyramid begin to breathe deeply in through the base chakra. As you inhale, point a clear quartz crystal at the chakra and visualize little sparkling rainbow-colored lights flowing from the crystal into the chakra. Do this ten times at the base chakra and then work your way up through every chakra to the crown, repeating the same procedure at each chakra. Next, bring the crystal up to your solar plexus and imagine that you are inhaling small rosy-colored lights into that chakra. If you could see prana, or life-force energy, it would look like these sparkling, dancing pink lights, so visualize them as clearly as you can. As you exhale, send the rosy lights out from the solar plexus to all parts of your body. First push them down to your feet legs, hips and stomach; next pull them up through your chest, neck and head; then bring them down into your arms and hands. If you wish, send them into the individual organs, including the brain. Do this until your entire gold body is filled with little twinkling rose-colored lights.

Remember . . .

When you have finished with the auxiliary techniques, always climb down the pyramid and bring your gold body back into the physical. After the above techniques you are liable to notice a dramatic change in the colors of your chakras as you climb back down the pyramid. Also, for several days after such a session you are likely to feel a strong, pleasant rush of exhilaration.

34

Reactivating the Immune System

Even traditional physicians are beginning to admit that our mind plays a tremendous role in maintaining an active, aggressive immune system. A strong, happy, healthy state of mind goes a long way toward sustaining a strong, healthy immune defense. On the other hand, depression and doubt can seriously undermine the immune system, and fear can shut down the immune responses altogether.

As mentioned earlier, one of the major problems with diseases such as cancer and AIDS is the fear factor. The minute a person is given a diagnosis of a potentially fatal disease, the fear of death wells up and begins to overwhelm the person's entire being, including the remnants of the immune system. As a result, whatever is left of the immune system is generally so paralyzed by anxiety that it stops functioning entirely.

In order to reverse these situations, traditional physicians are beginning to recommend that patients use a simple visualization technique to help reactivate their white cells. The technique involves visualizing white blood cells as little Pac-Mans, floating along gobbling up cancer cells, AIDS viruses, or whatever is pertinent.

The problem with the above technique is this: Is there anything wimpier than a Pac-Man? Can you seriously imagine a Pac-Man destroying anything as malignant as a cluster of cancer cells or an AIDS virus? Such toy creatures simply lack credibility in the real world, especially when a life is desperately on the line.

The kind of symbol we need for this type of meditation is a primordial, self-motivated, tireless, aggressive, ruthless killer that can effortlessly rip apart a life-threatening foreign organism and destroy every last remnant of it. As it happens, we all have a divine symbol built into our sub- and superconscious minds that fits this bill splendidly and is, in fact, intended for just this purpose. It is the Great White Shark. It comes to us from the Divine Mind and already has a preprogrammed, reactivating effect on our immune system.

We all have seen films of sharks in a feeding frenzy, hurling themselves at chunks of meat, slashing with their open jaws, curling their lips back to reveal rows of razor-sharp teeth biting down with several tons of force, and shaking their bodies violently as they rip off great masses of flesh . . . and then they come back for more and more and more.

This is exactly what healthy, fully functioning white blood cells are like. They are out to completely destroy any organism that interferes with our welfare, and they must do their work quickly and efficiently.

Deep meditation on the symbol of the Great White Shark can frequently reactivate a sluggish or damaged immune system.

However, this does not generally happen spontaneously — you must work with the symbol regularly and give it a chance to reprogram the parts of your mind that control the immune system. This repetition is a vital key to repairing and reactivating the immune response because by giving the super- and subconscious minds the same symbol over and over again, they can begin to build the concepts and the commands back into their DNA data banks and incorporate them into their current activities.

Begin by energizing your third eye with a crystal, a prism or a Power Tool. If you can find a photo or video of Great White Sharks, look at it until you are familiar with the sharks' appearance. Then close your eyes and build an image of a Great White Shark clearly in your mind. Visualize that shark swimming in a magenta ocean with sparkles of different colors playing through it — this is your bloodstream as it might look to your psychic vision.

Now visualize a few more white sharks swimming through this magenta ocean; then bring in more and more sharks until you have as many as you can picture. Visualize them cruising throughout the entire ocean (bloodstream) looking for one thing only — the intruder that is threatening your health and well-being. It is enormously helpful if you can also find a picture of your problem intruder — candida cells, pollen, cancer cells, the AIDS virus, Epstein-Barr or whatever, so you can make an accurate visualization.

Picture the hungry white sharks searching specifically for these invaders, finding them, attacking them without hesitation, and easily devouring them. Visualize more and more white sharks coming to participate in this feeding frenzy. When the frenzy is finished, imagine the sharks swimming back into the bloodstream to look for more of the intruders, finding them, and devouring every single one of them right down to the last shred. If you are working against cancer, visualize the sharks feeding voraciously on tumors, easily devouring them cell by cell until there is nothing whatsoever left of the mass. Then send them out to find and destroy any other masses that might exist. Remember that there is nothing that can stand up to the Great White Sharks — once discovered, foreign organisms have no real defense and they become easy prey for the sharks.

Caution: It is vitally important that the sharks home in on just one specific problem, otherwise they can damage other parts of your body. Clearly and strongly visualize that they eat one thing and one thing only — the specific intruder that is causing your health problems.

Repeat this meditation as often as possible. Every time you do it, visualize that you are adding more and more sharks to your bloodstream. Eventually you are liable to find that in your mind's eye — without even trying — you are beginning to see white sharks at odd moments during the day. This is an excellent sign; it means that your immune system is reactivating.

35

Reading DNA Memories

Precious memories, unseen Angels
Sent from somewhere to my soul,
How they linger ever near me
And the sacred past unfold.
Precious father, loving mother,
Fly across the lonely years,
An old home scene of my childhood
In fond memory appears.

In this chapter we will discuss another wonderful technique for triggering past-life memories, which involves picking up information stored in the DNA and bringing it up to our level of conscious awareness.

As mentioned a few chapters earlier, we all have two types of

DNA: our physical DNA, which we inherited from our parents, and our spiritual DNA, which our souls brought with us as we began this incarnation. Our spiritual DNA is like our soul's suitcase, carrying millions of pieces of past earth-life information, as well as information from our soul's sojourn on the finer planes.

Over time the two types of DNA blend together and influence one another, so our past-life memories are very much a part of who we are today. This spiritual DNA accounts for many of our likes and dislikes, talents and phobias, attitudes, tastes and major illnesses, because most of these characteristics have been formed throughout our many past lives and are simply continuing in this life. So in order to be successful healers, it is extremely worthwhile to learn how to bring up past-life memories for our clients as they work past chronic illnesses and try to regain past-life skills and knowledge. The following technique can make this difficult task much easier.

The Past-Life Train

Think of all the people and events in your current life, and notice the broad range of emotions connected with these memories. Your past lives are no different: there are, as the above song says, so many precious memories awaiting you, complete with rich emotions, sights, sounds, fragrances and thousands of other associations — providing you can retrieve them from your spiritual DNA. The Past-Life Train is a marvelous way to do just that.

The Past-Life Train Technique takes most of the work out of past-life meditation by bringing you some very valuable keys. These keys find and open past-life segments of your spiritual DNA, decode them, bring them up to the level of your conscious mind and display them for you in easy-to-understand pictures.

On the Past-Life Train you can view these pictures either from a slight distance (if, for example, the lifetime was traumatic) or from very close up; you can skip past several lives and look at only the incarnations that interest you the most; you can ask to see scenes from any specific lifetime; you can go back to favorite lifetimes over and over again; you can receive healing for traumatic past-life events; and you can stop when you want to.

Past-life knowledge is valuable in many ways: You (and your clients) can find unsuspected roots of present-day trauma and illness in past events; you can trace past relationships with people you are with in this life; you can remember past skills and knowledge; you can recall treasured lifetimes spent with spiritual teachers and Masters; and you can get a much fuller, four-dimensional sense of just who you are, where you come from and why you are here.

If all of this sounds fascinating . . . it is! So get ready for adventure: you have a first-class ticket to travel through the familiar scenery of your past. All aboard!

Using the Past-Life Train technique is easy, but you must carefully follow a few simple preliminary steps that will raise your kundalini energy to the extent necessary to access your spiritual DNA. Once again, here is a variation of the Master Meditation Technique.

Begin by placing a crystal or third-eye Power Tool on your forehead for about five minutes to energize your psychic centers. If you have difficulty seeing, you may lie down and put your crystal or Power Tool on your forehead for the duration of the meditation in order to boost your inner vision.

Breathe deeply and slowly through your solar plexus for about two minutes. This will prepare you for deep meditation by pulling large amounts of soul energy down into your physical body.

Next, close your eyes and imagine that you are rising up out of your physical body in a body of pure, rich gold light. When you are standing up in this body, visualize the physical landscape fading away, and in its place a beautiful green meadow beginning to shimmer and form. Fill in grass, flowers, trees, sky, birds and so forth. Notice that in the center of the meadow is a little old-fashioned train that consists of a locomotive and eight cars.

The engine is to your left, the caboose to your right.

Starting at the back of the train, the caboose is red; the next car is orange; the next is yellow; the next is white; the next is green; the next is blue; the next is indigo; the next is violet; and the engine is gold. As you might guess, each car corresponds to a chakra, and the gold engine represents the powerful force of your soul, which will pull your inner vision down to the level of the spiritual DNA.

To begin your journey, visualize yourself walking over to the little train and climbing up the back steps of the red caboose. Enter the car and take twelve steps, which will bring you to the front end of the car. Notice that all of the seats in the caboose are red. By walking through this red car, you have activated and energized your first chakra. Now take one step on the platform between the cars and enter the orange car. Walk through it in twelve steps, take one step between the cars, and enter the yellow car. Notice that the seats of each car match the color of the car: orange seats in the orange car, yellow seats in the yellow car and so on.

Keep walking through the cars, taking twelve steps in each one and one extra step between cars until you come to the violet car, which is the car you will ride in. Visualize that you have just entered this car: have a seat on the right-hand side. Imagine that a ticket from the Spiritual Masters is waiting for you on your seat.

The Journey

When you are settled, specify any particular lifetime you would like to see. You might ask, for example, to see an Atlantean life; a life as a healer; any life with your current spouse; or any life that is influencing a chronic or major physical problem. If you have nothing definite in mind, then just wait and see what comes up for you, but for your first few trips specify that you would like to see pleasant, strong lifetimes.

Now imagine that the train is starting to move, gradually

picking up speed. As you look out the window, visualize that you are entering a long tunnel; the light in the tunnel is deep violet, and at the end of the tunnel is a gold light. As the train passes through the tunnel and comes out into the gold light, the conductor will call out the place and date of the past life you are about to review (for example, Egypt, 3000 B.C.).

Look out the window and see what you can see. It is important to notice the sky: if it is blue and clear, this was a happy incarnation for you. If it is cloudy, there will be some disturbing events. If it is stormy and unpleasant, this life holds deep trauma.

Now you have two choices: You can stay on the train and go on into other past lives until you find one you like better, or you can reach up above your head and pull a cord to stop the train. When the train has stopped, pick up your suitcase which is behind your seat, go to the door, get out and wander around the landscape of your past-life memories. As you step off the train, your appearance will change to that of your former incarnation. In your suitcase is a mirror: pull it out and look at yourself. What gender are you? How old are you? How are you dressed?

Feel free to roam around; find your house and your family. As you ask questions, the scene will change. Ask to see both the best and the worst things that happened in this past life. Then ask to see your friends, family, spouse, children and so on. Ask to see important relationships from this incarnation, and ask whether you know any of the same people today. Inquire about your work, your skills, the lessons you learned and your teachers from this past life. Open your suitcase again for clues; it will contain special mementos that will jog your memories.

When you have seen all you wish, climb back up into the violet car, stash your suitcase behind the seat and sit back down. If you wish to see more past lives, wait for the train to start up and go through another tunnel (the tunnels are the connecting links between lifetimes). If you wish to end your meditation, let the train turn around and bring you back to the present; the conductor will call out "Home" when you are finished.

When you get home, exit the train the same way you originally got on: walk back twelve steps through each car, remembering the thirteenth step between cars. Walk from the violet car through the indigo, blue, green, white, yellow and orange cars, then walk through the red caboose and exit. Failure to do this last step will result in fragmented memories of the experience, so take your time and finish it up correctly.

Trauma

If the sky in a particular incarnation is stormy and you suspect you will encounter trauma, it is best to stay inside the train and view events from a distance. This will show you the problem without immersing you in it. Ask to see the traumatic event; ask how this old trauma affects you today and what triggers it. Ask why your soul chose this experience: was it to learn a lesson, to pay back karma, or to help a loved one?

If you see something really difficult to cope with, visualize yourself reaching up to the rack above your seat and pulling down a medical kit. Look inside for a prescription pad which will have written clues as to why this happened and how to heal it. Perhaps there will be a bottle of pills or a pile of bandages: ask the significance of each item. (These items can change from trip to trip, so be sure to look to see what's there each time you find trauma.)

If you feel cold from the trauma, move to the back of the car while the train brings you home. Visualize an old-fashioned wood-burning furnace in the back corner putting out a mellow, healing warmth. Bask in it and let it penetrate every cell of your being. You will feel better.

Be a Frequent Traveler

You can (and should) use the Past-Life Train Technique frequently: many important things will take time and practice to see, some will perhaps surface in your dreams.

If you have good clairvoyance you can even ask to see scenes of your astral activities between lifetimes. These will usually appear in fleeting glimpses while the train is in a tunnel.

You will find that the Past-Life Train is a wonderful source of knowledge, insight, nostalgia, and surprise . . . and the more trips you take, the better it gets.

36

Using the Akashic Records

For this chapter of our meditation series we will use a visual
aid to access the Akashic Records. On the back cover of this
book is a picture of a Power Tool called the Oracle. The Oracle is
a sort of window that connects with another interdimensional
window in the angelic realms. The angelic window connects with
the Universal Hall of Records, which contains detailed archives of
past, present and future events.

Who Needs the Akashic Records?

Many people think the Akashic Records are merely curiosities
that have little effect on their day-to-day lives, but this is not true.
Who among us could not benefit from the memory of our past-life
skills, knowledge, friendships, loves, triumphs and traumas?

Is there a particular period of history that fascinates you?

Would you like to be able to observe actual events that took place in Lemuria, Atlantis, Egypt, Palestine or Stonehenge? Would you like to watch the Buddha, Krishna, Christ and other great Masters when they were incarnate on Earth? Would you like to see the many beautiful Angels who live and work throughout our Universe?

If you or a client is experiencing chronic physical difficulties, what would it be worth to be able to tune in to the true origin of the problem, or to the thoughts of great healers — from this plane and other dimensions — who have encountered similar problems?

And what about those little mysteries in life . . . everyone has past events that they wonder about, wishing they understood why or how something happened. Wouldn't it be nice to get some objective answers to confusing episodes that influenced our lives either for better or worse?

Or perhaps you would like to explore life on other planets . . . the people, landscapes, healing and learning centers, scientific inventions, or possible solutions to many of Earth's problems?

When making plans for your future and that of your children, wouldn't it be useful to foresee the course of world affairs as they will be in ten, twenty or fifty years?

If you answered yes to any of the above questions, the Oracle can help you find the answers.

The Oracle not only allows you to read the Akashic Records, but it shows you the records on a much higher level than is normally accessible to us. Most psychics read the astral records, which are distorted by the constantly changing emotional currents of the astral plane. Reading the astral records is like trying to see a reflection in a pond that is constantly disturbed by waves and ripples. The Oracle, on the other hand, links to the higher vibrational records of the mental plane, which are much more accurate than the astral records. Reading the mental records is like looking away from the rippling pond and gazing directly at the event itself, without worrying about reflections and distortions.

The Angelic Spheres

The golden sphere depicted in the Oracle disk is one of many such spheres in the angelic realms. The spheres represent a highly advanced form of angelic technology; if you have the Rider tarot deck, you will see depictions of some of the spheres in the pentacles suit. Most of the angelic spheres are used for telepathic communication of one sort or another . . . they actively link people, places, planets and even dimensions. The particular sphere in the Oracle image provides a direct link with the Universal Hall of Akashic Records.

If you have worked with the angelic spheres between earthly incarnations, the Oracle picture will have a special appeal for you — some people will feel tingles up and down their spine or even bolts of electromagnetic current as they gaze at it.

Preparing to Use the Picture

The Oracle leads you through an exciting set of interdimensional windows. The higher your level of clairvoyance or clairaudience, the deeper you will go.

To set the scene for using the Oracle, imagine that you have come to Earth from another dimension: you have been living on this planet in human form while you experience the physical plane. Now, however, it is time to awaken and begin to carry out your higher mission, which is to help bring peace, light, and healing to this planet. You need to recover lost memories of your existence before you came here. You also need much additional information on a variety of topics. For most of you, this situation should sound right on.

If you have been reading these chapters in order, you already know the Master Meditation Technique that will raise your spinal energies and flood your cerebral meditation centers with the high vibrational psychic force necessary for interdimensional work. If you are skipping around, refer to Chapter 26, which discusses the

Master Technique in detail.

After you have done the Master Technique, hold a small quartz crystal or a third eye Power Tool up to your forehead for three to five minutes. As you do this, breathe in slowly through your solar plexus five or six times. Next, hold the Oracle picture in your hands and gaze into it for a few minutes. Notice exactly what it looks like . . . look at the details of the stone window, the roses, the ocean, the golden sphere and the Hall of Records.

Accessing the Records

Now close your eyes and visualize the Oracle picture as precisely as you can. Imagine yourself becoming smaller, walking right into the picture, and standing in front of the Oracle. From here you have three choices . . . for the best possible results try them all and see which one you like best.

First, you can float through the stone window and soar over the golden Sea of Time watching random scenes in the water as you go. This is a good technique for just browsing for information, similar to flipping through the pages of a book to see what is of interest. Before you float through the window you can specify whether you wish to see into the past, present or future. Then specify your topic, such as past lives, Atlantean crystals, future technology, life on Venus . . . whatever.

The second choice is to visualize yourself standing in front of the Oracle in your gold body: reach out both hands and lightly touch the sphere. The electromagnetic energy from your touch will activate the Oracle. Notice that it feels warm, and it pulsates. Now form a question in your mind regarding the information you need; then make your mind a blank screen and watch carefully for scenes to be projected onto the screen from the Oracle. If you are clairaudient, you may hear the information.

The third choice is to float in your gold body into the sphere and then through the doorway of the Akashic Library. Once inside you again form questions in your mind and wait for the answers to come to you. Or if you need a sort of screen to receive information, you can use the facilities: visualize books, magazines, newspapers, tapes, microfilm, TV, computers, and so on. There is also a card catalog, or you can look for a librarian and ask her/him what to do. The main thing is to hold your topic firmly in mind and allow the information to come to you in one form or another.

Notice that when you enter the picture, float through the window, go into the sphere, or walk into the Hall of Records you are intensifying your experience, branching out into four possible subdimensions. Is this exciting, or what?!

Finishing Up

When you have finished, come back through the window, or out the door of the Hall of Records, and out of the sphere, then exit the picture. Now return to the pyramid, climb back down the steps, and float your gold body back into your physical body. Breathe deeply to anchor yourself back on the earth plane. Failure to do these last steps will make it difficult to remember all of the information you gathered, so take your time and do it right.

Also, take time to write down all of the things you saw or heard, because a lot of the details can get hazy over time.

Past Lives

Past lives are not difficult to see; they are, after all, the very core of your being. Everyone can benefit in many important ways from past-life memories. Try asking the Oracle about some of the following things:

Your best lifetime; your worst lifetime; important past relationships that carry over into the present; past skills; past metaphysical work; past healing knowledge; lifetimes with Masters; past trauma that affects you today, and what triggers it; where you came from before Earth; the mission that brought you here; your mission companions.

When you are looking into a particular past life, ask to see the country where the past life took place; the date; whether B.C. or A.D.; the landscape around your home; what you looked like; your gender; your clothing; your house; the people you lived with; your feelings toward them; your occupation; high points of the lifetime; low points; how you died. This is slightly different from the other past life techniques given earlier, in that it filters the information through the Oracle from the mental plane, rather than up from the DNA or through the soul memory.

If you have good clairvoyance, you can also ask to see astral scenes of your activities between lifetimes — this is often just as informative as the physical incarnations because we continue earth projects on the astral plane between lifetimes, and we also prepare astrally for our work in future incarnations.

As an example of how it works, one question asked of the Oracle was regarding the Battle of the Little Big Horn, from the Native American point of view. Immediately the sphere showed the scene of each warrior riding into battle. It was perfectly clear what was in the mind and heart of each man . . . some were angry, some were frightened, some were worried, some felt trapped. Each man's state of mind was transferred into the mind and heart of the viewer in a flood of thought and emotion, making for a truly electrifying experience. A mental question is enough to change to the perspective of the Native American women, or the young Sioux boys watching the battle from afar, or the horses, or the cavalry men, or Custer himself.

Unlimited Possibilities

The Oracle picture can be your window to just about any time and place in the Universe: it just takes patience, practice and perseverance. Some days are better than others for accessing the records, so wait until you feel energized and clear. Then try it . . . I think you'll like it!

COPING WITH NEGATIVITY

37

Avoiding Nightmares

Nightmares not only take their toll on the physical body in terms of stress and subsequent loss of sleep, but they also damage the subtle bodies through a general lowering of vitality. Most healers and physicians agree that one important way to help sick people recover is to ensure a peaceful night's sleep, which is often difficult when the body is strained and not functioning normally. Many otherwise healthy people also suffer from nightmares to the point where they develop insomnia to escape them, or to subconsciously avoid uncontrolled astral projection.

In many cases these debilitating dreams can be avoided or ended altogether by simply putting greater quantities of white light around the sleeper. It behooves us as professional healers to inquire as to whether stressed-out clients are sleeping well, and to offer practical suggestions if they are not. The following methods are remarkably effective.

Pennyroyal

When made up as a flower essence, pennyroyal has the magnificent ability to immediately put a shell of impenetrable white light around a sleeper. Three to four drops of this essence under the tongue at bedtime will almost always ensure a good night's sleep. A bottle of pennyroyal essence sells for just $7–$12 and will last for many weeks. Look for the pennyroyal flower remedy in metaphysical bookstores, crystal shops, health food stores and the like. If there is none to be found in your area, it may be obtained from Pegasus Products, Inc., Box 228, Boulder, CO 80306, (303) 499-8434.

The Masters' Headband

Another inexpensive solution is a headband to cover your third eye and a throat guard to temporarily shut down your astral hearing. Begin by finding two small portraits of a Master such as Christ, Yogananda, Babaji, St. Germain, Mary, the Archangel Michael etc. If your pictures are large, find a photocopy machine that can reduce copy, or have a negative made of the portraits and then two photographic reductions. Pictures about the size of a fifty-cent piece or a quarter are best.

When you have both pictures ready, use a coin to trace a circle around each Master's face (so there are no sharp edges to poke your skin), and cut out the round portraits with small, curved fingernail scissors. Now cover both sides of each portrait with plastic laminating film — the kind that is probably on your driver's license or social security card — and trim the film so it too is round but slightly larger than the portrait, so that the edges stick together well. Next, find either a silk scarf or a small-sized version of the popular and inexpensive Chinese silk jewelry pouches that many people keep their crystals in. If you opt for the silk pouch, get an inexpensive jogging headband to go with it, and be sure the headband is not so tight that it leaves a line around your head, cutting off your circulation. The last thing you will need is some masking tape.

If you chose the silk scarf, at bedtime tape one of the Master pictures to your forehead over your third eye and tape the other picture over the hollow of your throat, with the Master facing away from your skin. (Use a small piece of masking tape because it pulls off relatively painlessly, without irritating the skin.) Then wrap the silk scarf around your forehead over the third-eye picture and tie it. The silk will keep many negative vibrations from reaching your third eye, and the two Master pictures will provide an even stronger line of defense for both the third eye and the throat.

If you are using a Chinese jewelry pouch, put one Master picture inside and lay the front of the headband inside the pouch flap; then snap the flap closed over the headband. The pouch should now hang down from the headband; simply position the band around your head so the pouch hangs over your third eye. Tape the second Master picture to your throat and go to sleep. Admittedly headbands and throat guards are awkward, but they generally put a fast stop to just about any kind of nightmare.

The Divine Mother's Cloak

This little meditation technique is a simple and effective safeguard. Just visualize the Divine Mother — whose power is absolute — giving you a long cloak with a hood. This cloak covers you from head to foot; it is roomy, soft and warm. The inside is royal or cobalt blue, the outside silvery like a mirror. Take a few moments to clearly visualize this cloak before going to bed; wrap yourself up in it, feel its warmth, snuggle up inside. Visualize the cloak covering your throat chakra and the hood covering your third eye. Then go to sleep confident of the Mother's protection. If you have visualized the cloak carefully, you will probably have the most peaceful night's sleep you've ever had in your life. The

Divine Mother's cloak will also give comfort in times of stress, illness, pain, confusion, emotional trauma and so on.

Finally, those who experience nightmares should not sleep within fifty feet of a crystal, Power Tool or any other device that can open and energize the third eye and throat chakras, making nightmares worse. Other things to avoid are power grids, pyramids or anything else that energizes the psychic centers. In cases of especially vicious nightmares, cut all meat, cigarettes, drugs and alcohol from the diet for a week, or longer if necessary. Also, keep your bedroom vibrationally clean: try burning sandalwood, cedar or sage incense just before bedtime. The high vibrations released by the burning incense will help ensure a good night's sleep.

38

Building an Auric Shield

Auric shields have long been used by Spiritual Masters to protect themselves and their students. Many lightworkers have found that as their spiritual energy becomes brighter and purer they become more sensitive to general negativity, and from time to time some lightworkers or their clients may become targets for psychic attack.

Earth's astral atmosphere is filled to overflowing with negative thought vibrations created by war, famine, disease, social and sexual violence, and unsettling emotions such as grief, depression, terror and anger. Everyone is constantly bombarded by these negative thought forms all day, every day. The Himalayan yogis estimate that at this point in time if you smudge your house to clear away unpleasant thought forms, you have only about fifteen minutes before it starts filling up with negativity again.

The planet's physical pollution is well known and is mirrored in the astral energy fields as well; industrial waste, exhaust from too many vehicles, and a state of general filth clog not only our own physical atmosphere but also large portions of the astral atmosphere as well.

For those who are trying to attain personal growth and spiritual enlightenment, such conditions are appalling. Our finely tuned psychic senses constantly pick up the surrounding negativity, making it extremely difficult to remain pure of mind, spirit and body, to keep our thoughts unclouded, to find clear telepathic airwaves, and to meditate in depth. The protective bubble of an auric shield helps eliminate these unsettling, unwanted, unseen influences and helps us maintain an inner state of purity, serenity and peace.

Auric shields put a protective energy bubble around people, pets, vehicles and homes. Such a shield screens all types of low frequencies and negative vibrations, preventing them from entering into your personal space. If you are a healer, placing a proper auric shield around yourself and your client during a healing session will greatly enhance the power of your work.

The most useful auric shield is a bubble composed of etheric, astral and mental light energy taken from your own auric field. The bubble wall is extremely thin, very much like a soap bubble, but its consistency is very tough and rubbery.

The surface of the bubble is reflective, like a mirror; any incoming negative, low-frequency vibration will bounce right off the surface. In the case of psychic attack, malicious energy is immediately returned to the sender. Also, during any kind of mental attack the bubble will become psychically soundproof, protecting you from hearing any negative thoughts coming your way. In addition, negative entities cannot see into the bubble, so you will be invisible to an attacker's psychic vision. On the other hand, the bubble allows all clean, clear, safe energy frequencies to pass easily through it.

The bubble is always perfectly centered around the person who is inside. There is no way to walk beyond its protective limit; it automatically follows right along with you as you move.

Forming a Bubble

Use the gold body and pyramid meditation technique to raise your kundalini energy. Then go to your special meditation spot. To form the shield, inhale deeply several times and visualize that you are pulling white light down through your crown chakra into your heart center. Then as you exhale, visualize the white light flashing out of your heart chakra and forming a perfect bubble of light all around you. Mentally specify that this bubble has all of the qualities of being thin, tough and rubbery; it is mirrored to reflect negativity; in case of psychic attack it becomes soundproof and repels psychic vision; you are always in the exact center of it; positive vibrations flow easily through the bubble's surface.

How large the bubble is and how long it lasts depends on you. As you exhale the white light, mentally set the size for it. For example, it can fill the room that your physical body is in, or it can go from your physical body to the far end of your yard, and so on. After specifying the size of the bubble, mentally put a time span with it. For example, "This bubble will remain intact for one day," or one week, and so on.

One word of advice when you are forming your bubble: be sure to concentrate on all parts of the bubble, not just the front part. Pay special attention to the top, bottom, sides and especially the back of the bubble as well, so a whole bubble is formed around you and not just half a bubble. (Half of a bubble is not much better than no bubble at all!) Then feel free to fill up the inside of the bubble with comfortable, pleasant, uplifting energy — perhaps rainbow light or the vibration of flowers.

The Follow-up

In the beginning, even if your thought energy has been strong and clear, your first bubble will probably last only a few hours. However, the more you visualize the bubble and the more practice you get creating it, the more permanent and stable your bubble will become. Because of this initial instability, at first you will have to reinforce your bubble about twice a day. When you get up in the morning and when you go to bed at night take a moment to briefly visualize the bubble shimmering all around you. That is all it takes to keep it intact and in place.

Forming an effective auric shield takes practice and perseverance. There is an art to building a long-lasting bubble of the right size and thickness, made of the correct subtle light energies, with good reflectivity. So focus very carefully when you are first forming your bubble. Then as you mentally renew your bubble twice a day, you will find that it gets easier and easier to visualize the bubble in every aspect. Soon, if you wish, it will become a permanent part of your auric field.

Bubbles are very useful in a variety of situations. Put them around your clients when you are working on them so they don't pick up random negative energy. Use a bubble during deep meditation and at night while you are out of the body and astral-projecting. You can also use a bubble in hotel rooms filled with strange vibrations; in hospitals filled with thought forms of agony, fear, worry, hopelessness, pain and death; and in bars filled with lurid, unpleasant astral entities. Bubbles are also highly desirable any time you are sick and your natural auric defenses are low.

When you are adept at forming your own bubble, you can use the same technique to place a protective shield around a loved one — even from a great distance — or around your house, your pet, or your car. Just pull white light down through your crown chakra and as you exhale, visualize the bubble forming around the intended person, animal, car, home and so on.

If you find yourself in a crowd, you will be able to mentally shrink the bubble down close around you, or expand it to include an entire gathering of family or friends, depending on the circumstances.

You will soon find that the practical uses of an auric shield are just about limitless, and you will understand why spiritual Masters put such a strong emphasis on learning this valuable skill.